THE NARROW TRAIL

"Chuck's grasp on the larger narrative of the story of God and His people drew me in, for which I am thankful. His admissions, scholarship, and pastoral heart dovetail into a beautiful offering that meets me in my weariness and encourages me for my daily struggle to live in truth and grace. And it will serve me—and those I minister to—well, until Jesus renews all things. Thankful for this offering!"

Mike Khandjian — Sr. Pastor, Chapelgate Presbyterian Church, Marriottsville, MD, and Author of A Sometimes Stumbling Life

"In the midst of great difficulty and adversity, The Narrow Trail by Dr. Ryor was refreshing to my soul. I am thankful for Chuck's reminders and reflections that points us squarely to the Lord Jesus Christ. I highly recommend The Narrow Trail and trust many will find their way to Jesus because of this book."

Tyler St. Clair — Lead Pastor of Cornerstone Church, Detroit, MI

"My friend, Chuck Ryor, has pastored in a variety of contexts, more than anyone in America I know. From church planting in the Bible Belt, student ministry on a State University campus, suburban youth ministry, and church revitalization on the west coast, Chuck has done it all. His experiences with Christians from all contexts and walks of life make him the perfect person to speak to Christians prone to wander off The Narrow Trail. I look forward to sharing The Narrow Trail with my congregation and am hopeful it will be a helpful resource for many. Chuck has a heart for those on the fence when it comes to their faith and has a desire to help them stay connected to the Lord and the church. We need The Narrow Trail!"

Dean Inserra — Sr. Pastor, City Church, Tallahassee, FL, and Author of The Unsaved Christian

"Using the apt metaphor of hiking toward a mountain peak, Chuck Ryor skillfully describes the ardor of the Christian pilgrimage. Knowing that many have given up the climb and even more are considering abandoning it, The Narrow Trail offers deep refreshment to keep us heading onward and upward. This fresh injection of hope is the balm weary travelers need."

Ray Cortese — Sr. Pastor, Seven Rivers Church, Lecanto, FL barriers are misunderstandings based on linguistic preconceptions, which prevent a fresh understanding of God's path to grace and peace.

This book is divided into three sections:

Tip #1—Never go alone

Tip #2—Know your limitations

Tip #3—Don't lose sight of the path

These rules also reflect the Christian's need for three things to spiritually prosper: genuine community, growing humility, and gospel clarity.

I've included a diagram that I have used to teach through the principles of spiritual growth contained in this book. My "Three Tips" address the role that these principles play in our spiritual development. God works through people (genuine community), in us (growing humility), and by His power (gospel clarity). All three of these spiritual propositions are found in and fortified by Scripture. I pray that these tips will serve as a spiritual guide for your climb of faith.

but a certainty based on the historic teaching about what Jesus has done for His children. I pray that by applying the three tips, you will find renewal in your faith and rejuvenation in your daily life. Along the way,

> **"The confidence in God's love I'm aiming for is not pie-in-the-sky, wishful thinking, but a certainty based on the historic teaching about what Jesus has done for His children."**

I'll point out the benefits of genuine community, growing humility, and gospel clarity, and I'll explain why so many have wandered from the church.

In one sense, all of us are wandering through this world. However, some of us are "natural" wanderers in the strictest definition of the word—we tend to venture away from norms. The constraints of others' expectations, or the humdrum conventional path, compel us to explore. Others of us are simply curious, and then inadvertently discover that we've lost our way.

The hymn writer Robert Robertson penned these words: "Prone to wander, Lord I feel it, Prone to leave the God I love. . ."[3] Whether you've lost sight of the path and need to find your way back to experiencing Jesus or are simply frustrated by your current view of Christianity, this book is for you. The Narrow Trail is a guide to keep you from getting lost along your faith journey. If you're drifting, it will lead you back to Jesus, who is waiting for you.

Great barriers exist, though, keeping some people with a heart to know God from looking to a church community as a source of hope and spiritual encouragement. Some of these legitimate barriers are based on negative personal experiences and historical evil by some churches. Other obstacles to embracing the three tips have been erected by a culture that has declared foolish what biblical and historical Christianity claims about human nature and Christ's mission.[4] As a communications professor and pastor, I have found, through my interactions with people of all backgrounds, that many church life is for spiritual thriving. The second marker of spiritual drift is a gradual adoption of an entirely different view of humanity's moral capabilities. The third and final indicator of spiritual struggle is that, for various reasons, a person changes their view about who Jesus was, what He came to do, and whether it's necessary to be a Christian to be in relationship with God.

Renowned pastor and author Eugene Peterson declared how he maintained a lifetime of fidelity in ministry: "I knew in my gut that the act of worship with the congregation every week was what kept me centered and that it needed to be guarded vigilantly—nothing could be permitted to dilute or distract from it."[2] Christians who shun any church community, adopt a self-aggrandizing view of human nature, and/or depart from a scriptural framework for their faith are in a spiritual predicament. The Old and New Testaments are unified about our need for spiritual community, growing humility, and accurate theology in order to truly know our Creator's character and attributes. Logically, if Jesus is divine in nature, we can see in His life and teaching what God is like and how He interacts with human beings. But it would be disingenuous of us to pick through Christianity's teachings, avoiding the ones that challenge our assumptions about who Jesus must be.

Of course, underlying many of these departures from Christianity is a cocktail of pain, brokenness, disillusionment, and social pressure. If Christian people have failed you miserably, if preachers have made you feel worthless, and if you have a loved one who isn't on board with following Jesus wholeheartedly, sometimes realigning your beliefs with the mainstream culture seems like the most pain-reducing thing to do. In the short run, you may feel that relief. But in the long term, if you're wrong about who Jesus is and what He's called His followers to do, there could be more pain and difficulty in store than you realize.

My goal for this book is to help you discover or rediscover a vibrant faith that is fully confident in God's love. The confidence in God's love I'm aiming for is not pie-in-the-sky, wishful thinking,

The human heart wants to be close to God. Saint Augustine wrote, "You arouse us so that praising you may bring us joy, because you have made us and drawn us to yourself, and our heart is restless until it rests in you."[1] In an era that has been termed "postmodern" (after the era of modernity) and "post-Christian" (after Western culture was primarily influenced by Christianity), those who want to know and follow Jesus Christ are often left wondering *how*. For the person who was raised in church but has abandoned the "practice" of Christianity, there are seemingly few relevant answers on how to rekindle one's faith.

One of the most pervasive methodologies for learning is the "Three Tips" paradigm. Online you can find three tips for just about every imaginable topic: boosting confidence, taking exams, losing weight, making money, etc. You name it and someone has created a way to simplify (or oversimplify) it. Reducing spiritual thriving to three tips might seem like such an oversimplification. I might agree with someone who felt this way, if not for the counsel from God's Word, observations from several other spiritual leaders, and my own Christian experience.

The Narrow Trail provides a "Three Tips" paradigm for experiencing God's grace through three important practices. Like the amateur hikers and climbers who are guided by those three hiking tips, we are counseled by Scripture to do the same: (1) Never go alone. (2) Know your limitations. (3) Don't lose sight of the path. Healthy Christian living happens when genuine community, growing humility, and gospel clarity are present. As we continue on this literary quest, we'll see that these realities must guide a person's spiritual journey for them to fully enjoy it.

For more than a quarter of a century, I have served as a Christian minister. I've worked with adolescents, the aged, and everyone in between. I have seen a pattern that leads to spiritual decline, or worse, indicates that people are moving toward abandoning Christian belief altogether. The first sign of trouble is that people stop engaging with their church and gradually adopt a diminishing view of how critical

> " **After many decades, it's apparent that, like a mountaintop, the closer I get to God, the bigger and more holy He gets, and the smaller and less holy I realize I am.** "

doing *that*. Shazam! Holy man. #notsomuch

When I started following Jesus, I thought that the farther along I got on the journey, the easier it would get. I've found the opposite is true. When I began hiking up the mountain, I had so much zeal and energy. But halfway up, I started realizing that many of my notions about this climb were erroneous. Christian television preachers try to convince us that Jesus died on the cross to make our lives easier on this earth. Just send them money and the rough places will magically be made smooth and the crooked paths made straight. (This is a deplorable application of a promise made to Israel's leaders in Isaiah 40:4, which reads, "*Every valley shall be raised up, every mountain and hill made low; the rough ground shall become level, the rugged places a plain.*"). TV evangelists say, "Exercise enough of your faith and you'll never be sick, suffer, or experience dark nights of the soul." Embracing this type of teaching early in my Christian experience set me up for disillusionment when the pain of life started to kick in. As I've advanced in years, I've discovered I'm not alone.

Don't get me wrong; there is great joy in walking with Jesus. There was great joy in hiking with my friend up Mount Wilson. The friendship and camaraderie made the journey bearable. His words of encouragement kept me going. The ongoing presence of a strong friend assured my safe passage through potentially dangerous terrain. As with my faith journey, the wisdom gathered along the mountain path has stayed with me. It helps me encourage others who venture out to do the same. One day, believers will reach the summit, where the Scriptures promise that there will be no more crying, dying, pain, or suffering. But in this life, it's "One foot in front of the other, bud."

Mountains. Life. God.

I was in so much pain, and I couldn't get my arms up far enough to make a "V." At best, I could make a "W," with my hands, which was appropriate because I was wiped out. My legs hurt so bad that I had to sit down while showering for the next two days.

I started hiking when I first moved to California. A friend offered me the conventional wisdom for beginners. These three tips are: (1) Never go alone. (2) Know your limitations. (3) Don't lose sight of the path. For my hike up Mount Wilson, I got two out of the three correct, which worked to my advantage. My big mistake was that I overestimated my ability to complete the hike. (My pride got the best of me.) That was a failure of ego. But if I'd been alone, I would have stopped at some point, and then it would've gotten dark by the time I got going again. In a panic, I might have left the path, and probably become lost. (Even in the daylight, I would have gone the wrong way several times, if not for my friend's guidance.)

I could've been more reflective before I agreed to this climb. For years I've known the following about myself: I don't like not knowing the road I'm traveling, and I hate not knowing how much longer I'm going to have to suffer. These are two inhibiting factors for a long hike on a poorly marked trail. In my perfect world, the National Park Service would put up clearly marked signs every quarter of a mile, noting that I was on the right path and had "X" number of miles to go. No such luck for hiking up and down Mount Wilson—just the promise that the peak is up there somewhere if you keep climbing, and that your car is waiting for you at the bottom.

Perhaps now you see what I mean about mountains being accurate metaphors for a life of faith. As a Christian, I began my journey of faith, believing that every step I took toward God was going to make me feel more holy. After many decades, it's apparent that, like a mountaintop, the closer I get to God, the bigger and more holy He gets, and the smaller and less holy I realize I am. Oh, I would've said I was small and imperfect when I started, but I didn't realize what that meant. Moral perfection seemed somehow attainable. God didn't seem that far away. All I had to do was stop doing this and start

Mountaintops are perhaps the most accurate metaphor for a life of faith. From a distance, mountain peaks look relatively easy to get to. However, the closer you get to them, the peaks seem farther away and more difficult to climb. This is one of the lessons I absorbed on my longer-than-expected climb up Mount Wilson, the Southern California peak closest to my home.

At 5,700 feet, Mount Wilson doesn't seem that high from a distance. It certainly isn't high compared to what professional mountaineers and avid mountain climbers are accustomed to scaling. But for a novice like me, it was more than I could handle. I suspected this was the case when I accepted the challenge from a friend, who thought that his turning 50 was an opportunity to show that we weren't "over the hill." I would have said no, but he is one of my best friends, and he owns the gym where I work out. Saying no would've been too big a bruise to my ego. But as we approached the summit, my groaning and incessant need for breaks eliminated all vestiges of my athletic pride.

"One foot in front of the other, bud." That was my buddy's mantra. I swear; if he hadn't been there, I might have stopped much earlier to camp for the night. However, by the time exhaustion set in, it was too late to go back and too dangerous to stay in the woods alone. (There are rattlesnakes, coyotes, bears, and mountain lions to contend with in the San Gabriel Mountains.) Besides, I had no idea how we got to where we were and zero sense of how to get back. That's an important thing to remember about hiking to the peak of a mountain; you still have to walk back to where you started.

When it came time to descend, I assumed the downhill portion of our day would be easier. However, with my feet already sore, my knees killing me, and my emotional resources nearly at their end, the return trip was, in some ways, more difficult than the ascent. What I thought I'd do at the end of the hike when I started the nine-hour journey was substantially different from what happened. I pictured a smile of satisfaction or my arms raised in a "V" for my triumph over the mountain. Well, I couldn't muster a smile because

INTRODUCTION

Walking the narrow trail is not walking with a narrow mind. A narrow path is a difficult one to walk. It often involves precarious dangers. It's crowded because the width is constricting. Because it's narrow, there's a tendency to consider walking on it alone. It may be even easier to imagine wandering over to a wider trail. Why bother with the narrow trail at all?

Jesus tells us why. He says that wide is the road that goes to destruction. And his path, the narrow trail, is one that leads to life. In spite of its difficulties, it remains both the safest and most long-term beneficial road. It's safe to say that Jesus was way ahead of him, but Christ's teaching was echoed in Robert Frost's classic poem "The Road Less Traveled": "Two roads diverged in a wood, and I—I took the one less traveled by, And that has made all the difference."

This book is written for the hungry soul who longs for clarity about their faith and real peace with God. Christian-identified people are wavering in their beliefs and abandoning involvement in church communities, for a wide variety of reasons. In a time when the church's reputation is waning, it's challenging for some to sift through the discouraging news to find the uplifting truth about who Jesus is and what He's done for us.

If you're seeking to better understand Christianity, or perhaps reconsidering what you believe altogether, this book is for you. Maybe you believe in God but you're uncertain about how to grow spiritually. Perhaps you used to attend church but have walked away. Or, you've faithfully attended church for years, but you still "don't get it." Many of us have been there or are there now. Whatever your reason for reading, I pray you will find rest for your soul, as Jesus promised in the Gospel of Matthew.

"Come to me, all you who are weary and burdened, and I will give you rest. Take my yoke upon you and learn from me, for I am gentle and humble in heart, and you will find rest for your souls. For my yoke is easy and my burden is light."
Matthew 11:28-30

S ometimes it takes a global pandemic like 2020's COVID-19 outbreak to make us rethink our mortality. We humans (Westerners in particular) think we are the most highly evolved species on the planet and the proverbial captains of our own fate. Humility is in short supply when the world seems to be turning in our favor, and we are comfortably ensconced in our cocoon of affluence and education. Then we get a dose of reality when a microscopic virus significantly disrupts our lives. That's when we rediscover our finiteness.

Human finiteness is part of the underlying crisis in contemporary Christian faith. Christianity is rooted in the Middle Eastern religion of Judaism. According to the Old Testament, the essence of being God's people is gathering together, humbled by God's power and our need for Him, yet secure in His blessings because of His covenant with us and His provision for the forgiveness of sins. New Testament Christianity is similar. Followers of Jesus band together for mutual support and humbly recognize their ongoing need for God and others. Jesus has provided a path to God because He fulfilled the need for an atoning sacrifice for human sin, sufficiently and with finality.

The concepts of community, humility, and the need for forgiveness run headfirst into individualistic cultures, where my experience has been that proud people seem unwilling to face the depths of their own brokenness. Most embrace the concept of evil in our world at some level. Generations of righteous movements have formed to oppose injustice and the evil of despots and oppressive governments. However, human beings naturally resist the idea of shining the bright light of righteousness into our own souls. Many of us fear that doing so would destroy us.

What is a narrow trail? When Jesus referred to a narrow road, he wasn't saying that people who walked along his path were narrow-minded. This is an unfortunate coincidence of culture and Scripture. Many in the West rightly are offended by those who are unable to see outside of their narrow scope of life. Therefore, people might rightly connect the offense of a narrow-minded person with one who was following Jesus' admonition to walk the narrow trail.

PREFACE

"Enter through the narrow gate. For wide is the gate and broad is the road that leads to destruction, and many enter through it. But small is the gate and narrow the road that leads to life, and only a few find it."

Jesus (Matthew 7:13-14)

TABLE OF CONTENTS

THE NARROW TRAIL
A Wanderer's Guide to Finding Jesus

© 2022 Chuck Ryor

Published in New York, New York, by Morgan James Publishing. Morgan James is a trademark of Morgan James, LLC. www.MorganJamesPublishing.com

Scriptures taken from the Holy Bible, New International Version®, NIV®.

Printed in the United States of America.

Requests for information should be addressed to:

Chuck Ryor
P.O. Box 70677, Pasadena, CA 91117
www.chuckryor.com

Morgan James BOGO™

A **FREE** ebook edition is available for you or a friend with the purchase of this print book.

CLEARLY SIGN YOUR NAME ABOVE

Instructions to claim your free ebook edition:
1. Visit MorganJamesBOGO.com
2. Sign your name CLEARLY in the space above
3. Complete the form and submit a photo of this entire page
4. You or your friend can download the ebook to your preferred device

ISBN 9781631954924 paperback
ISBN 9781631954931 eBook
Library of Congress Control Number: 2021930416

Cover and Interior Design by:
Franzine Mackley

Morgan James PUBLISHING Builds with... **Habitat for Humanity®** Peninsula and Greater Williamsburg

Morgan James is a proud partner of Habitat for Humanity Peninsula and Greater Williamsburg. Partners in building since 2006.

Get involved today! Visit
MorganJamesPublishing.com/giving-back

THE
NARROW
TRAIL

A WANDERER'S GUIDE
TO FINDING JESUS

DR CHUCK RYOR

NASHVILLE

NEW YORK • LONDON • MELBOURNE • VANCOUVER

"Chuck Ryor is a seasoned pastor who has walked with many people through their seasons of spiritual doubt and questioning. I believe that you will find *The Narrow Trail* full of timely wisdom and advice to help you in your own spiritual journey. Simple and straightforward, Chuck's tips are super practical and grounded in Scripture. Highly recommended!"

Dr. Paul Gilbert, PhD — Lead Pastor, Four Oaks Community Church, Tallahassee, FL

"For the seeker, the sleeper, the one fed up with religious grandstanding and showing off, for the disenfranchised and frustrated, for the one who after their latest wounding at the hands of another supposed follower of Jesus has walked away from the local church, Chuck Ryor is a winsome but clear guide for your journey back to the good way, the right path, or *The Narrow Trail*."

Ryan Williams — Lead Pastor, City on a Hill Church, Albuquerque, NM, and Director of Am I Called Ministries (amicalled.com)

"Chuck Ryor's mastery of culturally relevant story telling makes this a must read for every 'hungry soul longing for clarity about their faith' and every local church pastor. This brilliantly crafted work paints a realistic view of a Christian's journey in the 21st Century Western culture. Love, love, love the simplicity, captivating stories, and the 'Three Tips' Paradigm."

Tim Beltz — Retired Captain (USCG), Retired Executive Pastor, church consultant, and Author of *Charting the Course: 'How to' Navigate the Legal Side of a Church Plant*

"When Jesus commanded us to follow him, he meant to do so closely. Yet, at times we can find ourselves at quite a distance from the delight of his presence. In The Narrow Trail Chuck Ryor reminds us that what Christ calls us to he also enables in us, as we trust in him. His triad of Gospel Clarity, Growing Humility, and Genuine Community are worth the price of the book. Buy it, read it, live it, and then read it again."

Dr. David W. Hegg - Senior Pastor, Grace Baptist Church, Santa Clarita, CA, and Author of *The Obedience Option*, *When My Heart is Faint*, and *The Privilege of Persecution*

Tip #1: Never go alone

Spiritual health thrives in
genuine community.

H ow great of a mountain climber must you be when your nickname is "The Swiss Machine"? Ueli Steck's mountaineering career garnered him multiple awards. His achievements were legendary. He reached Mount Everest's summit (without supplemental oxygen) in 2012, and in 2015 he climbed all 82 Alpine peaks over 4,000 meters (13,100 feet) in 62 days. In 2019, he and a climbing partner attempted to summit Everest via the most difficult route. The BBC reported that this west ridge route had yielded more deaths than successful ascents. Yet, as most who climb professionally or compete at the highest levels in other areas, the challenge drove Steck to attempt a greater feat than he had accomplished previously.

Steck was a proponent of active acclimatization. When hikers attempt to climb Mount Everest, they elevate from base camp to higher base camp so their lungs can get accustomed to the decreasing oxygen at higher altitudes. Instead of just sitting in a tent, "the Swiss Machine's" experience had led him to believe that he could adjust faster if he was physically active at each higher level. Speed was a hallmark of Steck's style, and a few years previously, this resulted in a significant conflict between Steck and a climbing partner and a group of Sherpas. A violent confrontation resulted from the Sherpas feeling they were not being listened to by these advanced climbers. In a statement about the event, the Europeans claimed the Sherpas' pride was wounded because the Steck group climbed faster without their help.

Fast-forward to 2019. Before leaving for the Himalayas, Steck commented that he was stronger than ever. The man who was world renowned for his rapid ascents recorded on social media that he was climbing swiftly. One climbing partner, Tenji Sherpa, was having more trouble because he had contracted frostbite and could not train. However, Steck forged on alone, climbing to Everest Camp 2 and then up toward a nearby peak called Nuptse. On Sunday, April 30, 2019, the Swiss Machine began climbing at 4:30 a.m. with a French climber. However, before they reached Camp 3, Steck split off to climb Nuptse. Alone.

According to reports, when he was 1,000 feet below Nuptse's summit, Ueli Steck had fallen 3,300 feet to his death. A man nicknamed for his endurance and at the peak of his physical conditioning suffered because he climbed alone. While there is only speculation about what happened, the obvious benefit of having climbing partners is that they, if nothing else, offer a cautionary voice to aggressive sportsmen like Steck.

Ueli Steck is a legend in mountaineering. He set speed records for some of the most difficult climbs in history.

He died at age 40.

First Corinthians 10:12 warns us that if we think we are standing firm, we must be careful that we don't fall. Christians need community for connection, care, and discipleship. This book's first section will be divided into three chapters addressing genuine community. Obviously, we all must individually engage with God to grow closer to Him. However, it is equally clear from Scripture that Christians need others to show us God's love and care. We need social connection to experience the joy of community and friendship, and we need mentors to help us become fully devoted followers of Christ.

Chapter 1—The Individualistic Quandary: Why do I need to connect to a church community when all I need is within me?

Chapter 2—The Credibility Issue: How can I receive care from a church whose leaders don't seem to care?

Chapter 3—The Hypocrisy Problem: Why should I trust your efforts to disciple me if you don't practice what you preach?

People often say, "No one is perfect." And most of us would agree that an organization of imperfect people won't get close to perfection. However, for many people, the problem is less about the glaring mistakes and more about lack of confession and apology. Those practices, which are so much a part of Christianity, are strangely absent on many occasions. Each chapter in this section will highlight substantial issues that are real cultural barriers that keep people from pursuing Christian community. These same dynamics are causing many church members to wonder about the health of their communities of faith.

I realize that you might feel no need to be part of a Christian community. But if you'll read through this book, you might discover why being part of a church community is so critical for you. If you're a Christian who has stopped being part of a church community, have you discovered that you miss that part of your faith experience? I hope that as you read this book, you'll embrace its spiritual realities. There is a reason your soul may be longing for close and safe connection to others who will love and support you. You were made in God's image, and that's how He's lived for eternity.

ONE.

The Individualistic Quandary

A few years back, I was honored to attend a Navy SEAL graduation ceremony for a family friend. According to the safety regulations associated with the SEALs, I can't identify him by name. I'll refer to him as 003 because he was the third nephew born to my friend's family, and it has a James Bond feel to it. If you're unfamiliar with the Navy SEALs, this is how the U.S. Navy describes their mission:

> The Navy's Sea, Air and Land Forces—commonly known as SEALs—are expertly trained to deliver highly specialized, intensely challenging warfare capabilities that are beyond the means of standard military forces. Their missions include direct action warfare; special reconnaissance; counterterrorism; and foreign internal defense. When there's nowhere else to turn, Navy SEALs achieve the impossible through critical thinking, sheer willpower and absolute dedication to their training, their missions and their fellow Special Operations team members.[1]

Books and movies portray the intensity of the recruitment and training process used by the Navy to determine who gets to be part of this elite military unit. However, when I got a screenshot of 003's blistered heel, with the skin removed almost to the bone, it wasn't dramatized entertainment any longer (especially for his mom). Further stories came through the grapevine about him sitting in the cold ocean for most of the night, right up to the point of hypothermia. While BUD/S (Basic Underwater Demolition/SEAL) is the best-known portion of SEAL training, it constitutes only 24 weeks of a long and grueling process.

Graduation is an amazing accomplishment, and I've heard many stories about the challenges faced and overcome in the process of becoming a SEAL. My favorite story from 003's SEAL training is when, on the last night of "Hell Week," he and his fellow aspirants were paddling around Coronado Island in the middle of the night, cold and tired. They hadn't slept in several days, and all they'd eaten that day were notoriously bland MREs (vacuum-packed, military "meals ready-to-eat"). I'm not sure which would be worse for me, eating MREs or not sleeping for multiple days. They experienced both and much more. As they paddled and tried to complete their mission, another mission of mercy had begun on shore.

003's fiancée and brother both lived in nearby San Diego. While 003 was freezing to death, paddling in a rubber raft with his fellow candidates, the finance went to Taco Bell and bought dozens of burritos, chalupas, and gorditas. Then, in the middle of the night, the brother and fiancée began executing a plan whereby the brother would paddle out into San Diego Bay to deliver the food to 003 and his colleagues. Heading out on a surfboard by himself, the brother was spotted by SEAL security/safety vehicles. When he explained who he was, the officers let him continue on his mercy mission.

When he located 003 and his colleagues, he told them he was proud of them, reminded them that there were many people rooting for them, and urged them to keep pressing on—that they were almost to the finish line and shouldn't quit. Then he handed the bag up to his brother, told him he loved him, and paddled away. Though the food was appreciated, 003 noted that the words of encouragement were even more valuable to him and his fellow candidates at such a difficult time.

003 has been a Navy SEAL for a few years now, and he still can't give me much detail about what he and his teammates do. I suppose that's a good thing, because I would likely use that information as an illustrative story in a sermon or book. This guy is also one of the few genuine Christians in his outfit. I'm especially proud of Navy SEAL Christians because they humbly profess their need for Jesus in a testosterone-filled environment. All SEALs know that they can't fulfill their missions without others. SEALs aren't individualists. There are no "Rambos" in elite military units.

ME, MYSELF, AND I

Our individualistic culture of "self" compels people to put themselves first, declare they need no one else to succeed, and, by all means, make sure everyone knows how incredible they are. This independence certainly will make it difficult for them to connect with anyone in a church community (or see a need to do so), but it also makes them unavailable for others to connect with them. Comedian Jim Gaffigan joked about this self-consumed attitude, which he says is evidenced by having so many mirrors in gyms: "If I'm gonna be working out, I want to do something … like look at myself. I wanna look at myself as I work on myself. I should do a recording so I can listen to myself, while I look at myself while I work on myself as I leaf through my *Self* magazine: read how myself can improve myself. Maybe I'll go to my Facebook page and look at photos of myself—read what myself has written about myself."[2]

If you search online for the statement, "You can do anything you set your mind to," you'll find myriad articles and stories where people celebrate their individual accomplishments and use that saying for inspiration. Another popular internet subject is "Everything you need is already within you," which ostensibly sets the individual on a path to greatness, and possible success as the next self-help guru. Every generation has seen the ascendance of popular inspirational seminar leaders who capitalize on two characteristics inherent in all human beings: We are naturally self-centered, and we desire to see ourselves as better than others. Appealing to our individualism is one way that these seminars enable human beings to feel comfortable claiming that we don't need others.

Teaching others that "you can do anything you set your mind to" usually omits salient details that must be understood for a person to reach their goal. Chief among those is that others will have to help you, open doors for you, and inspire you when you feel like quitting. After all, wasn't that why you went to the self-help guru in the first place? Furthermore, proclaiming that a person has within them all they need to accomplish any goal neglects to mention human limitations. A short person with no natural athletic ability cannot play professional basketball at the highest level, even if he sets his mind to it 24 hours a day for three decades. He simply lacks what it takes to play in the NBA. He's never going to achieve his goal.

I'm not trying to be "Johnny Rain Cloud," but I want to point us toward the reality of how we were created and the truth of how we make it anywhere in life. Some people have been given talents that are the basis for their achievement. But they did not choose the family, city, or country into which they were born. And all of those natural talents were gifts from God. The nurturing of that talent is also something that takes place in conjunction with the gifts of other people. Family, friends, mentors, and heroes all play a role in enabling a person to reach full potential. But this potential might not be as high as someone might think, having been led there by a well-intentioned inspirational speaker. The unfortunate (albeit unintentional) by-product of the message for the hearer is a false sense of pride in one's individualism.

C.S. Lewis contended that foolish pride and unhealthy competition often drove human beings to want to achieve. He stated, "Each person's pride is in competition with everyone else's pride. It is because I wanted to be the big noise at the party that I am so annoyed at someone else being the big noise."[3] It is important to feel significant for the individual God created you to be. It's an insult to all of those who helped you get where you are to imply that your individual effort is how all of that came to pass. We're so quick to forget the critical role others have played in our journey.

> "It is important to feel significant for the individual God created you to be. It's an insult to all of those who helped you get where you are to imply that your individual effort is how all of that came to pass."

COMMUNITY AND COMMUNICATIONS

The academic pursuit of communications scholars is predicated on the notion that human beings exist in communities. The word "communication" is derived from the Latin word *communicare*, meaning to make common. Individual cultures and communities have verbal and nonverbal codes they use to pass along acceptable and unacceptable forms of thinking and behaving. As we communicate with others, we are faced with the inescapable reality that we're part of a world where we are interconnected whether or not we like it. No one is an island unto themselves, and no one gets where they are without significant help from others. Because Western societies tend to be more individualistic than communal, we might spin a narrative of success achieved through individual effort and accomplishment. But that is a charade.

The Dutch psychologist and sociologist Geert Hofstede pioneered much of the communications theory about the differences between collectivistic and individualist cultures. Put simply, collectivism is characterized by extended primary groups in which people see themselves as interdependent with others. Individual goals are secondary to group goals. By contrast, individualism emphasizes individual goals over group goals. These cultural expectations are learned early in life. Hofstede's studies revealed that cultures exist between these two poles of collective and individualistic.

Countries in the West, like the United States, Canada, and many European nations, ranked high on individualism, whereas countries in the Far East such as China, Hong Kong, Taiwan, Thailand, and others rank near the lower end of that spectrum.[4] Many other studies have been built on Hofstede's work, researching the upsides and downsides of each culture type. One need not be an academic to see the ease with which individualistic cultures could become overly self-interested, and how individuals within collectivistic cultures could lose an important sense of self.

Westerners (Americans in particular) have rugged individualism ground into their histories. The United States was formed as a union of states in rebellion to a king, with a Declaration of Independence reading, "We hold these truths to be self-evident, that all men are created equal, that they are endowed by their Creator with certain unalienable Rights, that among these are Life, Liberty, and the pursuit of Happiness." Some individualistic people believe that our inalienable rights mean that we can and do exist apart from responsibility to others.

The late American theologian A.W. Tozer addressed this inherent problem in humanity:

> "There is within the human heart a tough, fibrous root of fallen life whose nature is to possess, always to possess. It covets things with a deep and fierce passion. The pronouns my and mine look innocent enough in print, but their constant and universal use is significant. They express the real nature of the old Adamic man better than a thousand volumes of theology could do."[5]

We are by nature selfish, and few disagree with this assessment. Christianity is an Eastern religion founded in a communal society. The faith's hero is a Jewish carpenter who was the fulfillment of God's promise with the Israelites. Every Old Testament command is given in the context of communal living, which is why some of them make little sense to secular Westerners. When a person considers Christianity without observing the required commitment to be part of a community of believers, they aren't getting the entire picture of what it means to be a Christ follower, or why the Scriptures require connection to a church community.

THE INDIVIDUALISTIC COLLECTIVE

God sees us as individuals, but we're commanded to be part of a collective. Scripture says that He uniquely created each human being,[6] lovingly pursues relationships with individual souls,[7] and justly holds individuals responsible for their actions.[8] At the same time, the Bible describes how these individual beings were made to depend on one another. Furthermore, the New Testament calls Jesus's followers to emulate His holiness and humility by putting others' needs ahead of their own.[9]

There is a reason why God would be most glorified in an individualistic collective; He has always lived in one. The triune God is three distinct persons—Father, Son, and Holy Spirit. The Trinity has existed eternally in the godhead; a community that mutually serves one another and works in unity to bring glory to each other. Humanity wasn't created because God needed fellowship outside of Himself. As Yale theologian Miroslav Volf has stated, the Christian God is not a lonely God. As Father, Son, and Spirit, He is completely content in His own existence.[10]

However, that His glory might be seen and that He might have joy, God created human beings in His image and celebrated at the conclusion of creating man and woman by saying that what He'd done was good. He was pleased to create two people who needed each other, and that they would have progeny who would also be hardwired to need each other. In this mutual dependence and individuality, His glory and eternal attributes can be seen in us. The Father, Son, and Holy Spirit are interdependent and interpersonal. This was God's intention for human beings when He created them in His image. To live apart from community or think that you don't need others is to deny the essence of the ONE you were created to reflect.

However, knowing this to be true does little for those who have left the church and retain an element of emotional distrust of any Christian institution. It doesn't take too many bad experiences for us to determine that we'll no longer be gluttons for punishment. If I have a bad experience at a restaurant, I am unlikely to return. The old adage rings true: "We get only one chance to make a first impression." However, for many Christians, it wasn't a single event that caused their exit. Instead,

> "There is a reason why God would be most glorified in an individualistic collective, and that's because He has always lived in one."

what has driven many from the local church is a series of negative encounters with a church environment that perhaps spoke of God's grace but perpetually demonstrated little of it.

Most of us have endured seasons of doubt. We struggle deeply with sins or the hurt inflicted on us by others in our church. While Scripture says that Jesus won't break a bruised reed, church people can be less concerned about giving bumps and bruises to each other.[11] The late British theologian and author John Stott wrote:

> "One might say that the idle, the anxious and the weak were the 'problem children' of the church family, plagued respectively with problems of understanding, faith and conduct. Every church has members of this kind. We have no excuse for becoming impatient with them on the ground that they are difficult, demanding, disappointing, argumentative or rude. On the contrary, we are to be patient with all of them."[12]

In a genuine community, you have the freedom to be yourself. Unfortunately, many people believe that the church is the phoniest place in their world. While societal decorum discourages us from "emotionally bleeding" on others, the church is supposed to be a place of profound honesty, a place of encouragement based on patience and grace.

The apostle Jude wrote that the church was to be merciful to those who doubt.[13] Unfortunately, many whom I've talked with about why they've left the church said it was because of the marked lack of patience with each other. Some churches focus on the sins of others but seemingly spend little time focusing on their own. Such inconsistencies generate doubt regarding a church's ability to demonstrate the grace it preaches. Christian counselor and author Larry Crabb wrote:

> "Without a safe community, we will not own our brokenness. We will not provide others with the safety they

need to own theirs. Community will be a competitive,
demanding place where we feel the pressure to demonstrate
that God had done more work in our lives than He has."[14]

For the Christian, it is even more important to comprehend the necessity of genuine spiritual community. Without it, we will dry up spiritually. While you may have endured painful experiences that make you think this type of community doesn't exist, I assure you that God has a place for you. It won't be filled with perfect people, but it will be a community of people who are praying for greater comprehension of the gospel so they can love you well.

YOU ARE THE "BODY OF CHRIST"

You might have faced a disappointing experience at church and then run far and fast, away from the entire enterprise. However, according to Scripture, your efforts to distance yourself from the church may have been futile. The apostle Paul wrote, "Now you are the body of Christ, and each one of you is a part of it."[15] If you're genuinely a Christian, with the Holy Spirit living in you, you're a part of the body of Christ whether or not you know it or like it.

"Just as a body, though one, has many parts, but all its
many parts form one body, so it is with Christ. For we were
all baptized by one Spirit so as to form one body—whether
Jews or Gentiles, slave or free—and we were all given the
one Spirit to drink. Even so the body is not made up of one
part but of many.
Now if the foot should say, 'Because I am not a hand, I do
not belong to the body,' it would not for that reason stop
being part of the body. And if the ear should say, 'Because I
am not an eye, I do not belong to the body,' it would not for
that reason stop being part of the body."
1 Corinthians 12:12-16

The command to engage with your or any genuine congregation of Christ followers is merely a call to act like you already are in Christ. Theologians have always differentiated between the "visible" and the "invisible" church. The visible church is His physical presence: the local representation of Christ's body. These specific churches, whether they meet in homes, schools, or buildings with stained glass, should be governed according to Scripture. They are the means by which believers and others in today's communities experience Jesus's presence in the flesh and bones of the physical church.

The invisible church, by contrast, is all those in the world who are genuinely indwelled by the Holy Spirit. It is possible to be a member of the visible church (if not an official member, by declaration) and not be a member of the invisible church. Some of history's worst actors can and have been members of the visible church. For instance, many historical mafia figures claimed to be members of the visible Roman Catholic Church. However, their callous disregard for human life and law led many to conclude that they weren't members of the invisible church. Conversely, a person can be a member of the invisible church but not part of a local, visible church. However, they would be disobeying Scripture's commands. To live apart from who God has made you to be harms a local body and denies you the opportunity to experience and demonstrate His grace to others.

> "You might feel that the conflict and hypocrisy of other Christians validates your abandonment of the local church. I can relate to this on two levels. I've experienced hypocrites and have been one myself."

You might feel that the conflict and hypocrisy of other Christians validates your abandonment of the local church. I can relate to this on two levels. I've experienced hypocrites and have been one myself. This is where it gets difficult for the Christian with regard to the teachings of Scripture, which command us to deeply examine whether or not our sinful behavior is really any better than others'.[16] Jesus put it in more bluntly metaphoric terms when He said to get the log out of your own eye before you worry about the speck in another person's. That portion of the Sermon on the Mount is the one that includes the ironically popular refrain "Judge not, that you be not judged." Ironic because people often cite that verse to excuse their judgment and avoidance of judgmental Christians in a church.

> "Do not judge, or you too will be judged. For in the same way you judge others, you will be judged, and with the measure you use, it will be measured to you. Why do you look at the speck of sawdust in your brother's eye and pay no attention to the plank in your own eye? How can you say to your brother, 'Let me take the speck out of your eye,' when all the time there is a plank in your own eye? You hypocrite, first take the plank out of your own eye, and then you will see clearly to remove the speck from your brother's eye."
> **Matthew 7:1-5**

At the same time, I understand why it is difficult to re-enter Christian community after being hurt by people. I've been hurt by the church before, and when that happens my fight-or-flight instinct screams, "Bounce out the door and never look back!" But our first tip, "Never go alone," cautions me again that spiritual health thrives in genuine community.

PAINFUL PATHWAYS PRODUCE POSSIBILITY

When I was in ninth grade, my family vacationed in Hawaii. Most of our time was spent in Honolulu, on the island of Oahu. My five sisters and I basked in the sun and swam in the clear ocean water. As the only boy in the family, I had a time limit on sunbathing. My dad knew from experience that when his rambunctious son got bored, trouble wasn't far away. So, one Hawaiian afternoon, he grabbed me, and we ventured out for some guy time. We traveled to the other side of the island to snorkel in a coral reef formed by an ancient collapsed volcano. As you can imagine, the views inside this park were stunning. The former volcano was now open to the ocean, with a white sand beach on the shore. The shallow and the deep waters inside this national park were separated by a coral reef.

When we first entered the water, it was fascinating to snorkel around in the crystal-clear ocean and bump up against fish that were swimming in the shallow waters. However, after a while, the first section of snorkeling got a little boring; same fish, no coral, and limited intrigue. But if you were willing to make your way across twenty to thirty feet of jagged rocks, on the other side were deep waters with a variety of fish species and underwater plant life. The really interesting stuff, the fascinating organic plant life, and the big fish were in the deeper water. But it took an uncomfortable walk across sharp underwater rocks to get to it. Additionally, the deep waters were darker, colder, and in theory, more dangerous. But once you made the journey, the drudgery of the shallow waters would no longer do.

I have noticed a pattern in my decades of pastoral ministry. Some Christian people will begin attending a church, and like snorkeling in the shallow waters, they will find it fascinating. Nevertheless, once that honeymoon phase is over, they leave for the shallow waters of another church. I don't mean to imply that there are not legitimate reasons to leave a church and find a new one. However, if the causes for church-hopping are not theological, moral, or ethical (let alone having suffered abuse), but instead are as simple as being bored with the music or irritated by the quirks of certain people, you must ask if leaving your present congregation is the Christlike thing to do. Still, some perpetually leave churches. Instead of climbing over the difficult reefs before them to discover the more satisfying waters of relationship and community depth, they settle for less. These people opt to spend their life moving from proverbial beach to beach without ever progressing out of the safe, through the complex, and into great beauty.

It's easy for people to say, "I want Christian community." But the best part of Christian community requires some challenging and difficult walks into its deepest parts of the human experience. Those painful journeys are usually relational and often involve humbling oneself before another person, confessing our failures to one another, and resolving conflict with people we might be just getting to know. I have heard Christians wax eloquently about how difficult Christian community is, but then immediately leave a church for a new one as soon as the relational terrain got sharp and rocky. I have been one of these people! We can't wax philosophically that "church is messy," and then never stick around to work our way through tough times. Church isn't difficult if every time things get challenging, we leave. However, those who brave the painful moments of relational dissonance and cultural discomfort will receive the satisfaction of depth in friendships and shared community encounters.

One last thought about this: When we (pastors or members) leave our church communities for no good reason, except that we're restless and/or people have let us down, we're perhaps unknowingly acting in a way that countermands the gospel we proclaim. When we say, "I'll be in relationship with you if and only when you (a) meet my needs perfectly, (b) cause me zero emotional challenges, and (c) don't disappoint me, that is the opposite of the unconditional love of the gospel.

LESSONS FROM A FRIGHTENED CHURCH

The first-century church was dealing with a similar condition to what today's Western church faces. In the book of Hebrews, the author yearns to stem the tide of exodus from the community of believers. The Hebrew Christians were experiencing persecution from the society at large and from within their own families.[17] The cost of following Jesus was steep, often including physical beatings, imprisonment, or being outcast from your family and friend groups.

These trials were causing some who had publicly professed their faith in the resurrected Christ to recant their testimonies. The church leaders were calling believers to return to faithful engagement in the church fellowship to strengthen themselves. Like coals of a fire, Christ followers burn hot spiritually when closely connected with other believers.

However, it was easy then, as it is now, to discard the habit of making Christian community a central part of our lives. Prioritizing community connection often comes at the expense of our kids' activities, our recreation, or our vocations. As a pastor, I've had to work on Sundays for most of my adult life, so I didn't have to deal with Sunday sports leagues. But I do understand how tempting it is to prioritize the enjoyment and pride of watching our kids play or perform over having to wrestle them into the car to take them to church. Billionaire Warren Buffett famously said that the chains of habit are too light to be felt until they are too heavy to be broken.[18] Once Christ followers get out of the habit of making spiritual community a priority, they'll discover that when they need it most, they are either emotionally or relationally disconnected from others and cannot easily reconnect to them for encouragement. The writer of the book of Hebrews challenges us with this admonition:

> "Let us hold unswervingly to the hope we profess, for
> he who promised is faithful. And let us consider how we
> may spur one another on toward love and good deeds, not
> giving up meeting together, as some are in the habit of
> doing, but encouraging one another—and all the more as
> you see the Day approaching."
> **Hebrews 10:23-25**

Being part of Christ's body means being stirred up to love and good works. It means giving and receiving encouragement. Genuine, deep connection with a church family is one of the most important means of grace given for spiritual growth. If you're wondering how you can revitalize your Christian faith, the first step is to make it a priority to engage meaningfully with a church community.

It's the first tip of hiking: Never go alone.

CULTURE SHOCK AND CHURCH COMMUNITY

I spent one summer in graduate school assisting a professor with teaching an intercultural communications course to students from two very different countries: South Korea and Brazil. These students were in Florida for the summer to intern at Walt Disney World in Orlando, and the initial part of their intercultural experience was educational. The section of the course for which I was responsible was a discussion of the intercultural phenomenon known as "culture shock." Culture shock refers to the feelings of disorientation and anxiety that a person feels whenever they enter a new environment (particularly a cross-cultural one). But the principle applies to new jobs, relationships, cities, and virtually any substantial change to your living situation.

Whenever people arrive in a new culture, they'll go through predictable phases. According to researchers, those four phases can be best summed up using the "U-Shaped Curve" of culture shock (see diagram). The "U-curve hypothesis" was initially developed in 1955 by Norwegian sociologist Sverre Lysgaard. He described four stages faced by foreign exchange students. These four phases of adjustment

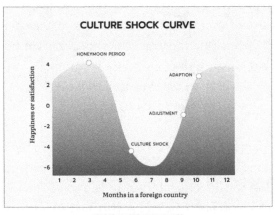

SOURCE: SVERRE LYSGAARD 1955

were originally known as the honeymoon period, crisis period, the adjustment period, and the biculturalism period. The stages have been renamed in many settings as honeymoon, culture shock, adjustment, and adaptation.

The honeymoon phase is characterized by excitement and optimism about the new context you're in. How long it lasts differs from person to person, but scholars speculate it's anywhere from six months to one year. Once you pass through the honeymoon phase, you make a quick descent into the culture shock phase. Here, it seems like what was amazing and exciting in the new environment has changed. What was fascinating and new is viewed through the lens of disorientation. Feelings and experiences that one can have in this shock phase include sadness, loneliness, melancholy, insomnia or excessive sleep, changes in mood, depression, feelings of vulnerability, anger, irritability, a sense of identity loss, a lack of confidence, and feelings of being lost or overlooked.[19]

With grit and determination, a person can rise above this inevitable crash into reality (after all, no situation is as perfect as it seems in the honeymoon phase) and ascend through a time of adjustment and, eventually, integration. Only after having toughed out the culture shock phase will a person feel they have adjusted and adapted to become part of their new environment. The application to one's church experiences (particularly if you find yourself continuously changing environments) is that perhaps the situation would improve for you in time. This may be an occasion where you should persevere through the culture shock in your current church. This season of struggle is where the Lord will be working powerfully in your life to form Christ's enduring character in you, and through it God will give you grace to love others, adjust (perhaps you have some unrealistic expectations?) and finally settle in as you adapt to where you have been placed by Him.

A LONGING FOR MORE

Perhaps you've tried to find a community that is faithful to what you believe, but you can never find one that features the kind of relationship connection that you want and need. This may be true if you live in a closed country (one where Christianity is illegal) or a rural town with one church. However, the vast majority of Westerners live within a short drive of multiple churches that can provide a place for them to grow in their faith. Often, when I've asked people about how they've tried to develop relationships in a church, they admitted they'd made minimal effort because they didn't have the time. Our longing for spiritual community can't be repressed. We were made for connection with others who know and love us as Jesus does, even as we struggle to love God and others as Jesus taught us to. And difficult people make it challenging to engage in a community where our innate needs will ultimately be met.

The apostle Paul longed for this connection. Consider, for example, his second letter to the Christians in the city of Corinth. Paul had a difficult relationship with this congregation and wrote multiple letters of correction to them. This would have made the relationship rocky, for sure. Few people's first reaction to critique or confrontation is impressive. Have you ever witnessed (on TV or in person) an intervention in the life of an addict? I've seen a few, and they're not pretty. I understand why. Those in recovery have to say goodbye to something that has, in many ways, been their friend in life's most difficult times. Addicts have come to love their substance more than the people in their lives, and when they are forced to choose between the two, they get angry. This was sometimes true of Paul's relationship with the Corinthians. But Paul didn't give up on them. Instead, he appealed to them as a father, hoping that they'd have genuine community with him.

"We have spoken freely to you, Corinthians, and opened
wide our hearts to you. We are not withholding our
affection from you, but you are withholding yours from us.

As a fair exchange—I speak as to my children—open wide
your hearts also."
2 Corinthians 6:11-13

The applications for making Christian community part of our lives are numerous. Of course, I would contend that living out these ideals is painfully difficult in situations where believers have been the object of spiritual or physical abuse, unrepentant racism, predatory sexual behavior, or other sinful events that have evaporated their trust in a church. In those circumstances it is entirely appropriate to distance yourself from the source of your harm. That said, those who don't fall into the abused category are only delaying the inevitable if we continue moving from church to church looking for that perfect place. On this earth there is not, nor has there ever been a perfect church. Eventually the Lord is going to help us resist our flight instinct. He will work in our hearts to endure with others through difficult times. As the Apostle Paul appealed to the Corinthians, we're being called to open wide our hearts to the Christians of the church we call home. My experience has been that the unwillingness of many of us to walk through difficult times shortchanges the work God wants to do in our lives. He wants to show us His grace through others.

Finally, assuming that you're not in the midst of a toxic church culture, your unwillingness to reconcile with difficult people (or any people) and live in an environment that is uncomfortable for you cheats others out of your presence. Because, after all, it's not ALL about you. Tip #1 is "Never go alone," which is true for you and for other people. Are you making it difficult for people to live that way?

TWO.

The Credibility Issue

I called it "the halfway point." Once we launched into it as a congregation, I knew that I was approximately thirty minutes from getting to go home. That was the significance that the Nicene Creed had for me in my youth. Having been raised in a zealous Roman Catholic household, mass was a weekly ritual never to be missed—even when on vacation. Of all my church experiences, none were more frustrating than interrupting a vacation at the beach to sit with strangers in a church I'd never attended before and would never see again. But even among total strangers, that halfway point brought relief. "We believe in One God . . . ." That was my wake-up call after the sermon. Several minutes later I would experience even greater elation when the "sign of peace" was exchanged among congregants. Mine was not joy born of the mutual affection of fellow believers, but of the knowledge that we were one communion processional from freedom. It was the horse racing equivalent of "and down the stretch they come!"

Although my parents were devout Roman Catholics, like so many children who grow up in religious families, I hated going to church. I didn't understand why we needed to dress up if God saw us naked in the shower. Besides, I reasoned, doesn't He have "Superman vision" and can see through our clothes? If God sees the heart, does it matter what we wear to church? Not that my heart desired church, but that was my point. God saw my lack of desire to be there—I don't think the tie fooled Him.

Additionally, I was not excited about going to church and fessing up to the angry "man upstairs." That was because throughout each week, I didn't say "no" to the many temptations that face young people. In my youthful understanding, I had to work hard to get right with God. I perceived my heavenly Father as having a hair-trigger temper and limited patience for weak people. I was a sensitive kid, so my misperception about God made perplexing the idea of a tender and long-suffering God.

Another reason I hated church so much was that amid the standing, sitting, and kneeling of Catholic Mass, I would grow physically weary. To get some relief during the kneeling portions, I liked to rest my butt on the pew seat behind me. My parents would have none of that. "Sit up straight!" they commanded. I know that isn't exactly suffering at the highest level, but it was a bit much for my folks to wake me up at the crack of dawn on the weekend and expect me to be mentally alert *and* practice good posture. Sunday, fun day! My Baptist and charismatic friends have church horror stories of another kind. I'll give my Catholic parents this: At least the church service was only an hour. Comedian John Mulaney quipped that this could be a marketing strategy for the Catholic Church: "It's an hour!" I have friends who would spend entire Sundays at church and then have to come back on Wednesday night.

In addition to these puzzling childhood church experiences, I had my own journey of rebellion and failure. I felt alone in the world, navigating the issues of my own heart and mind with seemingly few concrete answers. When my teen years rolled around, I launched into often getting drunk, starting on my 13th birthday. It was as if I was declaring, "Welcome to teenage hell, Mom and Dad!" It got worse for the next couple of years. I'll spare you the details. Lots of hospital visits. Multiple trips to court. Parental nightmares.

By the time I got to college I had already sown most of my wild oats and was on to the bigger philosophical questions of life. My journey of genuinely walking with Jesus began during my senior year of high school, when a girl I was interested in invited me to her church. She was Pentecostal; I was Roman Catholic. Let's just say our childhood worship experiences were different. Her youth group was something I'd never seen before. Great music, tons of kids my age, and, most of all, an energetic, basic Christian message that I had not previously comprehended. That night, in response to a challenge to follow Jesus because He would forgive me of past, present, and future sins, I humbly, gratefully, and after many false starts, finally gave my whole heart to Christ.

As I finished high school, I began to grow in my faith as never before. What an odd thing it was to head for college like so many others, intent on enjoying freedom from my parents' authority. Weirdly, my rebellion was 180 degrees from that of most others. It's common for those who grow up in church to get to campus, join a Greek house, get drunk a lot, and skip church altogether. All the while, they lie to their parents about attending church while away at school. Instead, I joined a nondenominational Christian student group, stopped drinking, and lied to my parents about going to Catholic mass (I attended Protestant churches).

When I discovered that I could be at peace with Jesus—and that the peace He offered included an assurance that I was guaranteed to spend eternity in His presence, I wanted everyone to know about this.[1] My journey with Jesus got off to a zealous start that resulted in some immature and, frankly, odd behavior. For instance, my freshman year in college my dorm floormates and I were permitted to paint anything we wanted on the hallway wall just outside of our room. Most painted pictures of their favorite beer can or movie poster. I painted a really bad picture of Jesus on a cloud with a bible verse above it. For most of the year when I was in the room with my door was closed, I could hear people in the hallway remarking how incredibly weird the Christian was who did that.

In my defense, my learning curve was fairly steep (more climbing imagery for your enjoyment). I grew up having memorized the Lord's Prayer and the Nicene Creed because we recited them each week in the Roman Catholic Church liturgy. However, my biblical knowledge was secondhand. I couldn't quote Scripture, and I certainly couldn't tell you where a verse was located. I was biblically illiterate because, like most Catholic kids, I hadn't grown up singing Bible memorization songs. That might have been a good thing, given the case of one of my best friends, Ken. His fundamentalist Baptist church taught him to memorize Revelation 21:8 by singing it to the tune of "Frère Jacques": "Revelation, Revelation, 21:8, 21:8. Liars go to hell, liars go to hell. Burn, liar, burn. Burn, liar, burn." That is a twisted childhood teaching strategy. It has practical upside for me, though. Every time we go out to dinner, I tell Ken I forgot my wallet, and then I get a song.

Steadily I began to learn Scripture, study theology, and interact with various Christian groups. Eventually, I established firm convictions about what I believed. Most importantly, while I sought wisdom from lots of people, I came to my own conclusions apart from my parents' influence or anyone else's pressure. While Christian community assisted me in understanding my faith, it was critical that I know what I believed and why I believed it. Over the years I weaved my way through multiple denominations and theological systems to arrive where I am today. Three decades later, I now describe myself as a multidenominational Christian who wants others to know how they can sustain spiritual growth over the long haul of life. Continuing in faith in the midst of an increasingly skeptical culture isn't easy. The circumstances in which people find themselves pose many challenges to our faith. However, any hike is worth the climb if, at its conclusion, you get a beautiful view of the world.

Why do people scale Mount Everest? Is it the challenge? Is it a hobby? Is it to boast of the accomplishment to others? Whatever the reason for climbing the highest peak on Earth, one thing is certain: It won't mean much if they don't make it back alive. And each year, several people die climbing Everest. Presumably, no one sets out to summit Everest thinking to themselves, *I hope I die on this climb. I want my body to remain on the mountain forever, frozen in solid ice, preserved for all time.* But that is what happens to most who die on Everest. (It is dangerous enough to descend the world's biggest mountain without bringing a frozen body with you. So, the dead are often left behind.)

The Christian journey poses unique challenges, making it difficult for many of us. This is increasingly true in the West, as studies indicate that the fastest-growing religious demographic is a statistical group categorized as having "no religious affiliation." There's a growing segment of our population that chooses to ignore their previously held religious tradition and/or orthodox theology.[2]

Many in this generation now deem their childhood beliefs too restrictive or out of step with modern culture. Add to that the credible accusations of child abuse against multiple denominations of Christianity, and it gets even more challenging to defend the church.[3] As a pastor and college professor, my experience with self-described "spiritual but not religious" people indicates that they believe in some sort of higher power, God, or spiritual plane. Perhaps you put yourself into this category. Many have a profound lack of trust in organized religion and have concluded that the Christian church is a source of great trouble in the world.

THE CHURCH HAS A CREDIBILITY PROBLEM

No doubt there have been failures at the highest and lowest levels of the Christian church. My

IN THE U.S., NUMBER OF RELIGIOUS "NONES" HAS GROWN NEARLY 30 MILLION OVER THE PAST DECADE*

Estimated number of U.S. adults, in millions

178 million

Christians

167 million

68 million

39 million

Religiously Unaffiliated

2009

2018-19

Source: Aggregate Pew Research Center political surveys conducted 2009 and January 2018-July 2019 on the telephone. Population figures calculated from U.S. Census estimates of the adult population.
"In U.S., Decline of Christianity Continues at Rapid Pace"

PEW RESEARCH CENTER*

point in defining this as a credibility problem is that the church's failures (many of which have never been admitted to or apologized for—at least not until the press got wind of them) have hamstrung the proclamation of the gospel. Whether accurate or not, the church's less-than-stellar reputation hinders its appeal to those not already part of it, and to many who've abandoned it. In the age of global, split-second communication, the church's glaring sins are magnified as never before, and it's having a negative effect.

My academic concern is that a communication problem is widening the gap between the formerly churched and the Christian community. My pastoral concern is that because of this, many Christians who have left the church are curtailing their spiritual growth. Some have abandoned identifying as Christians altogether. Others now claim that they don't need to be an active part of a local church to be a healthy Christian. I disagree and have written this book, in part, to encourage believers to reengage with a vibrant Christian church.

Also, I'm hoping that Christians who sporadically attend a church will realize the spiritual benefit of a closer connection to other Christians. To paraphrase my friend Dean Inserra, a fellow pastor and author, there is more to being a Christian than going to church once a week—but there certainly isn't less. Communal worship is a critical part of our collective church life, and it's vital for a believer's spiritual thriving. One can exert all sorts of energy working to better humanity, but Scripture makes clear that you need others to minister to you and others need you to be there for them. Logically, corporate worship can't happen without each other. Otherwise, it would be individual worship. And in spite of what you may think, there are Christ-honoring, people-serving churches that are concerned about correcting the problems that exist in our world.

Jesus said that we're to love each other so that the world will know we're His followers.[4] One reason for the challenge facing churches is that a new generation is discovering the support role that churches played in prolonging the scourge of American slavery and its aftereffects of racial discrimination and injustice. While there was

> "**One can exert all sorts of energy working to better humanity, but Scripture makes clear that you need others to minister to you and others need you to be there for them.**"

slavery in New England, it was largely theologically conservative, Southern Protestant churches that justified oppression in their preaching, and/or promoted a church culture that stayed silent while their Black brothers and sisters suffered under chattel slavery (complete with the sexual, emotional, and physical abuses).

One of the heroes of my church's theological tradition is Jonathan Edwards, whose influence on the Great Awakening and education has earned him the historic title of America's greatest theologian. However, as Jemar Tisby has written, "Although Edwards remains a significant figure in American religious history, his significance must also include the fact that he compromised Christian principles by enslaving human beings."[5] The challenge for us is that people are assessing the church's ability to care for them by watching if we care about the oppressed. Many of us have sins to confess and turn from regarding racism and injustice. Many religious groups need to do the same and pursue reconciliation.

Some Christians are reluctant to apologize for the sins of kin or countrymen who have come before them. I believe it mirrors the gospel when we do. The essence of the Christian message is that Jesus took responsibility for sins that weren't His own. He did this to bring about reconciliation between people and God. Jesus didn't have to carry out that mission; He willingly chose it, out of love for His children and loving deference to His Father. As theologian John Stott wrote in his classic The Cross of Christ: "So then, although he knew he must die, it was not because he was the helpless victim either of evil forces arrayed against him or of any inflexible fate decreed for him, but because he freely embraced the purpose of his Father for the salvation of sinners, as it had been revealed in Scripture."[6]

Is it possible that out of love for our neighbors, we can be compelled by Christ's Spirit to apologize for our forefathers if it would promote healing and help people see the gospel more clearly (taking on the sins of another to bring about reconciliation)? Is such an apology necessary to repair the church's reputation? I think so. I've heard arguments against this position. Some say Jesus absorbed our guilt but didn't confess to our sins, as if He did them. Whatever the argument, the optics are not helping the church's reputation with outsiders. Are we really arguing about whether or not we have to apologize? Shouldn't fallen sinners have their default mode set to apology? I believe so.

To their credit, some theologically conservative denominations have, in recent years, made further efforts to distance themselves from their troubling history with racism and white supremacy. That's a terrific thing, because a new generation of socially conscious Christians is intolerant of any perceived injustice in the church, or passive tolerance of its existence in culture. The church's credibility is at stake because its reputation can keep people from believing that we actually care about people. This is one important reason why the apostle Paul wanted elders to have a good reputation with outsiders.[7]

RELIGION AND POLITICS

America's melding of church and politics has had a particularly toxic effect on the reputation of the church and its conversation with culture. Imagine a nightmarish Thanksgiving dinner with relatives with whom you disagree about everything. That's what it feels like to be in the United States right now. The association between church and politics is perhaps the most daunting problem facing the Western evangelical church.

The conflation of Republican politics and evangelical Protestant Christianity has created a social climate where those who disagree with conservative policies could easily infer that they'd have to embrace the "Grand Old Party's" platform to be a Christian. Westminster Seminary's Dr. Carl Ellis has said, "There is no salvation in politics. We can speak politically, but Christians cannot be married to one particular political movement. If you marry politics, it will pimp you."[8]

> " **There is no salvation in politics. We can speak politically, but Christians cannot be married to one particular political movement. If you marry politics, it will pimp you."**
> – Dr. Carl Ellis

To be fair, that pendulum swings both ways. I've talked with politically liberal Christians who cannot stand to be in the presence of someone with a conservative political worldview.

Some progressives have declared, "I'm done with conservative Christians." Regardless of your politics, a dismissive and impatient attitude toward your brothers and sisters in Christ is completely inexcusable for the genuine Christ follower. With the Western world so politically polarized, an overly fervent association with one political party effectively shuts off conversation with Christian brothers and sisters on the other side of the political spectrum. This mix of religion and politics divides the church in a way that brings further disgrace to the name of Jesus Christ. Sadly, the process of making enemies out of those who aren't enemies makes some people feel more secure. In 2018, pastor and author Tim Keller wrote this in his op-ed for *The New York Times*:

> "While believers can register under a party affiliation and
> be active in politics, they should not identify the Christian
> church or faith with a political party as the only Christian
> one. There are a number of reasons to insist on this. One
> is that it gives those considering the Christian faith the
> strong impression that to be converted, they need not only
> to believe in Jesus but also to become members of the (fill
> in the blank) Party. It confirms what many skeptics want
> to believe about religion—that it is merely one more voting
> bloc aiming for power." [9]

The concern of many Christians like me is that Christian political coalitions have willingly forfeited their biblical voice on a host of critical issues, for fear of offending their non-churched coalition partners. Issues of social justice and righteousness are brought up by Christians from one political party but ignored by Christians of the other, all out of fear of losing influence within their own coalition. Both conservative and liberal Christian organizations are equally susceptible to being pressured into supporting a political agenda or leaders who oppose Christian ethics. In coalition politics, you may get a seat at the table of power, but you'll be expected to have table manners.

This gets even more dicey for Christians when they support leaders who are openly rebellious to Scripture's commands. Author David French wrote, "The view that good policy can redeem immoral acts treats a policy statement as a form of baptism—it washes away the person's sins."[10] For religious political groups, the ends often justify the means. The late Michael Cromartie was even more blunt. Cromartie, who died in 2017, was previously vice president of the Ethics and Public Policy Center and a man *Christianity Today* once characterized as "a consigliere for conservative Christians in the nation's capital."[11] Cromartie explained his perspective on conservative evangelicalism's relationship to Ronald Reagan's presidency: "Sure Reagan used Evangelicals, but Evangelicals used Reagan, too, to get access so they could be heard on their issues. Every politician uses Evangelicals because they want their votes. It's part of the political process."[12]

Many Christians find that admission troubling. "What? The church being used for political ends?" I'm concerned that many conservative and liberal politically active Christians are not focused on the church's reputation. Their first concern seems to be their party's political agenda and their small piece of that agenda. Their secondary concern (maybe) is whether or not people who need to know Jesus will be able to see through the haze of heated partisan rhetoric to view the beauty of the gospel of God's grace in Christ. Some have been crass enough to equate their political party with the Christian mission.

Both Christian conservative and liberal political action groups have valid concerns that must be addressed by the state. However, I suspect that these groups' underlying motivation is a thirst for political power. That's particularly true when they claim to be Christian but can't or won't sit down to hear the concerns of Christians with a different party affiliation. That's a long way from "They'll know we are Christians by our love."

DISTRUST OF INSTITUTIONS

A young businessman once told me he didn't trust organized religion. I replied, "That's good news for our church, as we're not very organized." I knew what he meant. It's not difficult to see the church's current and historical flaws and distrust churches in general. From a media and communications standpoint, the rise in the distrust of religious groups is certainly related to the abundance of information that is available to this generation. Before the internet, we wouldn't have the massive amount of credible information that reveals the church's failings, which for far too long have been hidden in the dark. Perhaps you've abandoned the church because you've seen these very public sins. You might ask, "Why bother being involved with churches? How could I possibly receive care from people who don't seem to care about morality?"

All of this public scandal and heavy-handed political influence has chased many people away from Christian churches, specifically evangelical Christian organizations perceived to have money and political power. Maybe you're one of those who walked away for this reason. It's not surprising, as reputable survey after survey tells the story of a younger generation of Westerners not trusting institutions, including religious institutions.[13] While America is not a "theocracy" in a technical sense, there is a cultural theocratic state that is sensed by many. With little or no allegiance to institutions, a new generation of church skeptics won't tolerate incremental change about racism, sexism, or abuse. They're either turning to non-traditional churches or they've ceased attending church altogether.

It's easy to find the flaws that mar the church's history. It's much more difficult to discover the many great things that the church is doing and has done for humanity. Two substantial reasons for this lack of information about the good work the church has done are (1) good news is rarely in the news, because good news doesn't result in "shares," page clicks, or viewers as does bad, sensational news, and (2) for all their myriad faults, Christian churches have, for the most part, avoided tooting their own horns. After all, Jesus was crystal clear on this point when He told us not to practice our righteousness in front of others to be seen by them.[14]

Critics of religion in general and Christianity in particular have declared that Christians have done more damage to the world than any group in history. However, British theologian Simon Smart declared, "The idea that most of the wars of history have been caused by religion is demonstrably false. The vast majority of wars have been conducted in the pursuit of profits or power, or waged for territory or tribal supremacy, even if religion has been caught up in those pursuits."[15]

Sociology professor Alvin Schmidt wrote in his book *How Christianity Changed the World*, "It has become 'politically correct' to fault Christianity for authoritarianism and repression, a faith that promoted fanaticism and religious warfare while impeding science and free inquiry."[16] Schmidt's volume details extensively how, over 2,000 years, the Christian church has been responsible for stemming the tide of plagues, poverty, and persecution. For all of their bad press, Christians and churches around the world have built hospitals, orphanages, schools, and shelters for those less fortunate.

But those accomplishments are easily ignored in the dismissive, Western, largely Anglo subcultures where religious thought is mocked. There is no defending the sins of Christians, and in the global communications world there is now no hiding that the church and its leaders are by nature a mess. What shouldn't surprise anyone is that it has always been this way with Christian churches. One glance at the New Testament Corinthian church confirms this. Sexual scandal. Parishioners suing one another. Drunkenness during church gatherings. Chaotic worship services that were making outsiders think the church was out of its mind. The first-century church had it all.[17]

However, somewhere along the way, people started expecting perfection from churches. The first-century church leaders (who wrote the New Testament) made it abundantly clear that they were utterly sinful and in dire need of redemption. Their plight was so bad that the eternal Son of God would need to die in their place to enable them to stand before a Holy God. Even with the help of Almighty God by the indwelling power of His Holy Spirit, when all these broken people gathered in church, they were prone to make a mess. This is as true today as it was then.

Unaware of this being the normative condition of the Christian church, an increasing number of folks are facing disillusionment about being part of one. Many doubt if it's necessary for spiritual thriving, while others deny outright they need a church community to be a healthy Christian. If either of these are you, I'm here to encourage you that you're not alone in your discouragement about others' behavior (it's why Jesus died for us). Scripture says that Christians are not naturally "good people," and it can be a challenge for us to commune with each other. Nevertheless, by cutting yourself off from a gospel driven, scripturally focused church, you're depriving your soul of the spiritual community it needs to survive.

THE PANDEMIC, YOU, AND THE CHURCH

We live in a broken and sick world filled with people affected by sin and struggle, just like us. The church is but a spiritual hospital. And if you stuff a church full of spiritually sick and broken people and spiritual health care workers, you're going to end up with some disappointments, and, sadly, some tragedies. Any evil and injustice happening in the church must be called out and condemned by its leadership. When needed or required by law, punishment and recompense should be made. However, some of what happens in the church is the simple by-product of being around sinners (like you and me) who need God's grace.

In 2020, as the global coronavirus (COVID-19) pandemic swept over civilization, one of my best friends was on the front lines fighting. He is an emergency room physician, and one of his biggest concerns was for his own family, as he was regularly exposed to people who had the virus. Every day he would come home from the hospital knowing he was potentially a carrier of the virus. That's the fascinating thing about hospitals; they're full of sick people. Even the doctors charged with restoring patients' health can (because they get sick) put those patients at risk. A truly loving place can from time to time be a dangerous place to go.

Contrast my friend's caring hospital with what happened at another facility in 2017. A Denver health care worker and hospital were sued when this nurse intentionally infected her patients with the deadly hepatitis C virus. It was reported that the healthcare professional placed contaminated needles into the veins of unsuspecting people. What a horrific thought that you could go to a hospital and a single crazy person could turn that place of healing into a center for pain and suffering. Still, when considering hospitals, I don't know anyone who would say the presence of bad hospitals precludes the possibility that great ones exist. Nor should the existence of terrible hospitals keep anyone from going to one in an emergency. (They'd simply hope that their local hospital was one of the good ones.)

Churches are like hospitals. They are filled with broken people trying to help broken people. Sometimes these spiritual hospitals have been utterly dangerous places for people to visit. Metaphorically speaking, there are people who have never experienced a good spiritual hospital and have determined it's worth the risk to avoid them altogether. My hope is to encourage you that there exist churches which are genuinely aspiring to become more like Jesus. However, I don't want to disingenuously communicate that those churches are anything but imperfect, including the ones where I have served.

My current church has many areas where we fail to serve our community well. We aspire to be better and to more effectively reflect the glory of Jesus, but you'd be disappointed if you came to our church expecting perfection. The deeply human reality in which we all live is that God has called us to be part of a Christian community that is imperfect. He has factored our sin and struggle into His plan for congregational life. Genuine community is a place of great imperfection, but it's still the best place to be for our own spiritual health. Trusting God in this way is not easy, especially if we've had bad experiences, some of which have been cruel or abusive.

I've been hurt by the church as a parishioner and a pastor. Unfortunately, I've also doled out plenty of

> **"Genuine community is a place of great imperfection, but it's still the best place to be for our own spiritual health."**

hurt to others through my selfishness or insensitivity. Apologizing to people has become an increasingly large part of my life. Whether it is the social media message I got from a person I traumatized when I was an attention-hungry teenager or the mother of a young person in my youth ministry whom I let down by not caring for her son, I've been told again and again that, as a person and pastor, I have let people down. Time after time, I have agreed with this assessment and apologized.

You may ask, "Why on earth would I go anywhere near your church?" Well, I'm not intentionally failing people; I'm just a human being, like you. I may be a little further ahead on life's climb than some people in my church. (I certainly have stumbled on more trails and fallen more frequently.) But I'm not at the summit calling down instructions on how to navigate the route perfectly. That is no excuse for my bad actions or inaction. What I offer to others as an ambassador of Jesus is the grace that I desperately need, day after day after day.

THE GOSPEL PRODUCES THE GRACE TO FORGIVE

According to Scripture, those in Christ have been forgiven for all of our sins against God. Therefore, we no longer need to be defensive when confronted with our own failures. Any accusation against me is probably accurate. I have sinned many times, through thought, deed, and failure to act when I should have. The good news of Jesus Christ is that these sins against God have been forgiven. As a Christian, I have been charged to forgive others, just as God has forgiven me through Christ. I've also been called to humbly ask for forgiveness from others.

"Therefore, as God's chosen people, holy and dearly loved, clothe yourselves with compassion, kindness, humility, gentleness and patience. Bear with each other and forgive one another if any of you has a grievance against someone. Forgive as the Lord forgave you. And over all these virtues put on love, which binds them all together in perfect unity."
Colossians 3:12-14

My father had a plaque in his office, which read: "My friend is not perfect, nor am I ... we suit each other admirably." That's what we should expect from our church experience. If we make it about people failing us (or fearing that we will fail them), we'll miss an opportunity to help accomplish Jesus's mission for our world. Through the work of Jesus Christ, God has and will continue to graciously walk among us even as we sin and struggle. He has promised He will never leave or forsake His children. God is there for us, even when we disappoint Him. Yet so many who claim the name of Jesus communicate the opposite by failing to associate with some other believers. This refusal to be present with imperfect Christians who you don't like or aren't maturing fast enough for you, is the opposite of what God does through the gospel. A relationship of conditional love says, "I will walk with you only when you change. I will stay with you only if you always act perfectly. Otherwise, I'll abandon you because you are a disappointment." Jesus says, "I'll endure patiently with you while you struggle to better reflect my holy attributes."

When we realize that we're living contrarily to the gospel, we need to ask why. Scripture says that we love because He first loved us.[18] Therefore, when we don't love our brothers and sisters in Christ enough to endure with them because they're broken and sinful and "unworthy of our presence," we reveal that we haven't truly comprehended God's grace in our lives. We experience real change when the truth of God's Word goes from our head to our heart. When God's love moves us internally, we can demonstrate it to others. We're motivated to love God by our growing comprehension of His love for us. When we're not exhibiting the character of our Savior, the problem is our lack of real, heartfelt comprehension of what it means to be God's children. Therefore, our first action must be to reengage with God, so we are moved again by His amazing grace to love Him and others.

Brennan Manning wrote, "It takes a profound conversion to accept that God is relentlessly tender and compassionate toward us just as we are—not in spite of our sins and faults (that would not be total acceptance), but with them. Though God does not condone or sanction evil, He does not withhold His love because there is evil in us."[19] Genuine community is supposed to remind us of God's faithful, patient endurance. When we fail to show patience to others, it communicates more loudly than our hypocritical words ever could.

Caring for people as Jesus cared for them requires that we have experienced His care. That's what is so confusing about seeing churches, church people, and church leaders act so carelessly toward others who are hurting and broken. We are supposed to experience God's care in the proverbial hospital that is the church. Genuine community should provide an environment where a person experiences Jesus's grace in real time. Instinctively, we know we need community, and we cry out for care when we're hurting.

The challenging truth is that every church community on earth is a broken one. This is how God reminds us of our need for Christ in us, as well as our need for others and their need for us. Unfortunately, those of us raised in the individualistic Western culture have been convinced that we have all we need in and of ourselves. When things are going well, it is easy to think this is true. When life's pressures and disappointments bear down on us, we quickly discover our need for others.

THREE.

The Hypocrisy Problem

John McCain is perhaps best known for his thirty years of service to his country as a senator from Arizona. After his death in 2018, more information emerged about his military service in Vietnam, and his five-and-a-half years of being tortured in a North Vietnamese POW camp. On October 26, 1967, Lieutenant Commander McCain, a Navy pilot, was shot down in his Skyhawk dive bomber. He was taken prisoner and suffered unfathomable abuse at the hands of his captors. Having broken several bones in his arm and leg, he received poor medical care. Even though he was injured, he was kept a prisoner of war, in violation of the Geneva Convention.

His cruel treatment in the first years of captivity almost broke him emotionally. He was severely beaten, tortured, and pressured continually to violate the oath he took as an American serviceman. Additionally, he battled dysentery for over a year. Dysentery is a bacterial infection of the digestive system, which produces chronic diarrhea. This type of disease, according to the World Health Organization and the Centers for Disease Control, annually takes millions of lives in developing countries, half of them children.[1] Dysentery results in bloody diarrhea. Its victims lose weight until they lack the strength to go on living.

McCain eventually recovered from his illnesses but spent much of his time in a cell by himself. This solitary confinement was a torture tactic used to break POWs. While in captivity, he and his fellow prisoners developed a communications process whereby, even though separated by concrete walls, they could stay emotionally connected. Amazingly, without being able to talk, the men created a new language. They would attract their neighbor's attention with a greeting tap and then wait for a response. After that, a single tap was an "A," two taps was a "B," and so on up the alphabet. This elaborate system of tapping on the wall was not written down, but memorized. It was the only way the prisoners were able to talk. McCain said that was the key to their survival.

However, communication with other prisoners (even tapping) was forbidden. "I had the singular misfortune to get caught communicating four times in the month of May of 1969," McCain recalled. "They had a punishment room right across the courtyard from my cell, and I ended up spending a lot of time over there." Here are insights from John McCain about the key role communication and relationships with others played in his survival:

> "As far as this business of solitary confinement goes—the most important thing for survival is communication with someone, even if it's only a wave or a wink, a tap on the wall, or to have a guy put his thumb up. It makes all the difference."

> "Communication with your fellow prisoners was of the utmost value—the difference between being able to resist and not being able to resist."

> "Communication primarily served to keep up morale. We would risk getting beat up just to tell a man that one of his friends had gotten a letter from home. But it was also valuable to establish a chain of command in our camps, so our senior officers could give us advice and guidance."[2]

This last bit of wisdom stands out to me. These prisoners of war, men who were suffering and trying to endure intense pressure to betray their country, required leadership and support from senior officers. These phenomenally tough guys knew they needed others for strength and direction. This is exponentially true for Christians in the West, who may increasingly be pressured to recant what they believe. In the absence of a Christian community that fosters and strengthens a scripturally directed faith, our beliefs will morph into a Christianity that looks more like the culture around us than it does the church of the New Testament.

Again, the first of the Three Tips is "Never go alone." In this first section, we've made the case that we need connection, and we need to be cared for. And we've been commanded by God to make a church connection. It is also apparent from Scripture that the primary way we develop Christlike character and endure life's difficulties (including pressure to deny particular teachings of Jesus) is being led and challenged by mature Christians. Spiritual health thrives in genuine community.

> " In the absence of a Christian community that fosters and strengthens a scripturally directed faith, our beliefs will morph into a Christianity that looks more like the culture around us than it does the church of the New Testament."

Any believer can grow spiritually by making a deep, genuine community in a local church the bedrock of their Christian growth. In this chapter, we'll contend that growing in Christlikeness happens through relational contact with other Christians in a church environment. Theologian and author Michael Horton wrote, "Nothing is more sanctifying than another person in our life. They are good at holding up mirrors, when we had quite different images of ourselves."[3] We need others to thrive as Christian believers.

For argument's sake, let's assume you could make it without Christian community (I think I've shown you cannot live without others, let alone other believers). While you may think you can live without other believers, the unvarnished truth is that the Christian life is not all about you. Being a member of Christ's family implies that others need your presence. Rick Warren's best-selling book *The Purpose Driven Life* began by stating, "It's not about you." And when it comes to Christian community, I would add, "It's not ALL about you." We need the encouragement and support from others; the body of Christ is as much about your needs as it is anyone else's.

However, for every person who erroneously thinks she can survive spiritually without this support, there are others who need her. Aside from that, Jesus has commanded us to actively love our brothers and sisters in Christ. Sure, Jesus says we should love all of our neighbors, and the church should focus some of its energy on meeting the needs of the most desperate among us in our community at large. However, on the night He was betrayed by Judas Iscariot, arrested, and led off to be crucified for the sins of the world, Jesus drove home some lessons He'd been sharing for three years with His inner circle.

His disciples were sitting around the Passover supper table when, unexpectedly, Jesus got up, grabbed a bowl of water and a towel, and washed their feet. This was a symbolic act that had significantly more meaning at that time than it does now. Sandaled feet and dusty roads made for an unpleasant combination when it came time to sit next to others for a meal. In most wealthy homes, a house servant would wash the feet of the people who came into the home. It was one of the lowest positions in society. Hence, when Jesus assumed that role for His friends, He taught them that He expected them to do the same for each other. He tagged this demonstration with these famous words about the genuine community that believers are supposed to have:

> "A new command I give you: Love one another. As I have
> loved you, so you must love one another. By this everyone
> will know that you are my disciples, if you love one
> another."
> **John 13:34-35**

This poses a challenge to the contradictory notions of the independent Christian. Jesus said a big part of demonstrating that you are a Christian is your public connection to and love for your Christian community. But for some, this is seen as theoretical because so many of the church's leaders don't seem to practice this ethic themselves. Certainly, we should expect our leaders to walk with integrity before God, but Jesus's teaching is relevant whether or not some leader somewhere fails to embody it. Our spiritual health is at stake if we fail to lovingly offer ourselves to others. That's why we say, "Never go alone."

THE HYPOCRISY PROBLEM

To be willing to let others lead you spiritually presumes that you think you need leading, and that you trust the person who is doing the guiding. Ever since I became a follower of Jesus, high-profile Christian leaders on radio or television have given critics of the faith plenty to mock. More than anything, televangelists' peculiar antics have created the general impression that Christianity is for unstable people. Put another way, many non-churched people have imputed to all churches the distrust they have for the scandalous church celebrities they read about in the news. Some of today's professing Christians behave erratically, raising the question, "Why would I follow anyone that untrustworthy? Why listen to anyone who clearly doesn't practice what they preach?"

> **"Our spiritual health is at stake if we fail to lovingly offer ourselves to others. That's why we say, 'Never go alone.'"**

The "Prosperity Gospel" TV preachers and their local church disciples promote a false Christian message that purports to deliver earthly riches in direct response to sacrificial giving (to them, of course). The grand poo-bah of this health-and-wealth gospel heresy reportedly has a net worth approaching a billion dollars and an airplane hangar full of jets—including a $20 million Citation X and a Gulfstream V purchased from American film director Tyler Perry.[4] Several televangelists have made public appeals to their audiences so they could purchase expensive private airplanes. However, it isn't just their ministry travel lavishness that belies the gospel of Jesus. They live like kings and business moguls 24/7.

When seeing this, many inside and outside of the church think to themselves, *Doesn't this contradict Christian teaching about* sacrifice? If Jesus and His disciples lived without a home or an abundance of money while they traveled and ministered, isn't that the pattern that these so-called Christian leaders should emulate? The short answer: "Yes, it is." The longer answer gives us deeper insight into this travesty masquerading as Christian maturity. The primary error and obvious hypocrisy of the leaders of the "Word of Faith" movement is their lack of faith. They think they are demonstrating great faith in Bible verses that celebrate the creation of wealth when, in fact, they are demonstrating a lack of trust and belief in the basic principle that Jesus gave to us: "It is more blessed to give than to receive."[5] Jesus says there is greater joy and greater fulfillment in giving our things away than in keeping them.

In their blinding greed, these televangelists missed the greatest biblical truth about abundance: The purpose of great wealth is to be a great blessing. The apostle Paul assured the Corinthians that they would be enriched in every way so they could be generous on every occasion.[6] James, Jesus's half-brother, wrote that religion that God our Father accepts as pure and faultless is this: to look after orphans and widows in their distress and to keep oneself from being polluted by the world.[7] King Solomon, who was arguably one of the wealthiest men who ever lived, recognized the spiritual danger of money and possessions. He wrote:

> "Two things I ask of you, Lord; do not refuse me before I die: Keep falsehood and lies far from me; give me neither poverty nor riches, but give me only my daily bread. Otherwise, I may have too much and disown you and say, 'Who is the Lord?' Or I may become poor and steal, and so dishonor the name of my God."
> **Proverbs 30:7-9**

To quote Solomon or other Old Testament promises about God's material blessings without simultaneously recognizing the dangers of having too much is pastorally negligent. For a minister to amass wealth from the sacrificial offerings of people and hoard material goods is dishonest. Implying, by virtue of your practice, that having a mansion on earth or a private plane is the summit of joy, without emphasizing the greater joy of giving more of it away, is spiritual deception at its most manipulative. Meanwhile, the viewing public watches and asks, "How could I learn anything from these people, who don't practice what Jesus taught?" It's hypocrisy for a minister to teach, "Have faith in Jesus, and He will bless you with money," and then lack the faith to give away more than you keep. I don't have a problem with wealthy people who earn their money. But if so-called ministers collect your charitable contribution and build a personal financial empire, you should have a problem with that.

> **"I don't have a problem with wealthy people who earn their money. But if so-called ministers collect your charitable contribution and build a personal financial empire, you should have a problem with that."**

GENUINE FOLLOWERS GENUINELY FOLLOW JESUS

As offensive as some misrepresentations of Christianity may be, they do not eradicate the truth of what Jesus says about our need for others' assistance and support as we follow Him. Some professing Christians are really bad at imitating Jesus, but that should not surprise any self-aware Christ follower. That doesn't lessen the negative impact of religious impostors or soften the painful blows of religious leaders who have done and said things that have harmed us. I get that. But to be a follower of Jesus, we need to know that our Lord has taken into account the foibles of fools and sincerely wants our best when He commands us to receive from our church *and* give of ourselves to it.

The spirit of our individualistic culture is that we are independent, strong, and competent people who prize our autonomy.

People who resist authority are celebrated in the lore of popular culture. Whether they're shunning their parents' rules or telling the boss to "take this job and shove it," popular culture loves the rebel. The Scriptures say that the human heart is deceitful and rebellious by nature, which makes the task of "following" Jesus difficult for all.[8] The nature of being His "disciple" is to walk behind Him, learn from Him about the world and how we're to love it well, and emulate His words and actions. The core of being a follower of another person is to submit to their directives, which sits poorly with our human nature.

Mentioning words like authority or accountability often elicits responses akin to fingernails on a chalkboard. The notion of submitting to anyone or anything conjures up images of slavery and oppression. Yet there is no escaping the New Testament teaching that Jesus was God in human form, and that to be a follower or "disciple" of Jesus Christ is to submit to His definitions of truth, justice, love, and whatever else He had to say about life and faith. The foolishness (and, at times, evil) of some who call themselves Christians makes it difficult for many to associate with Christ followers. This is why some people distance themselves from any local church community, just like they avoid certain relatives at family reunions. However, real Christians love their neighbors, even the difficult ones who act like fools. If we act lovingly only toward those who are perfect, we'll never have to love anyone (given that true love requires sacrifice). But Jesus loved us unconditionally and commands us to do the same.[9]

A follower of Jesus follows Jesus. And today's followers of Jesus are commanded by Scripture to have other Christians walk with us for encouragement and to sharpen our faith. We all need accountability, and part of Christian growth is hearing the truth from Christians in our church community. How do I know that the local church is so central to being a follower of Jesus? Because most New Testament letters were written to local churches and not to a formless, ungoverned, "invisible" church. Even the book of Revelation has specific addresses from God to particular local churches. The New Testament letter to the Colossian church makes clear that our spiritual growth as Christians is a group project:

> "Let the peace of Christ rule in your hearts, since as
> members of one body you were called to peace. And be
> thankful. Let the message of Christ dwell among you richly
> as you teach and admonish one another with all wisdom
> through psalms, hymns, and songs from the Spirit, singing
> to God with gratitude in your hearts."
> **Colossians 3:15-16**

BELONGING, BELIEF, AND COMMUNICATION THEORY

Worldwide demonstrations for justice confirm that a new generation longs for a purpose that connects them to a community of people who also have purpose. A new generation of Christian believers is influenced by the notion that they are here on earth to glorify God by seeking justice and serving the needy. People want to belong, and political movements provide community for those with shared values. One can find great friends among others who embrace their concern for the environment, social justice, or other issues. These causes inspire human beings to discover community.

Yet what often goes overlooked is how values drive belonging to a group. If I am not a proponent of gun control, it is unlikely that I would be received well by a gathering proposing restrictions on handguns. If I am a registered Democrat, I will be looked upon suspiciously by those with conservative political values. Add to this confusion a culture that pushes back on the idea of universal absolutes, and you'll find it difficult to have a justifiable reason for telling anyone "no" or "wrong." That is, unless the standards of right and wrong are established for that particular community.

In the sociocultural tradition of communications studies, there is ample scholarship to demonstrate culture groups' power to create meaning, values, and practices through communication. One of the founders of this field of communications studies was anthropologist Dell Hymes. He held that for cultures to communicate and flourish, they need a common code, communicators who know and use the code, a means of communicating, a setting for the communication to take place, a message form, a topic, and an event created by the transmission of the message.[10]

When I study this formulation of community and culture, I think about its application to today's church. Hymes was not saying that culture's influence was a bad thing, but rather that this is how human beings manage to live together. This is congruent with the biblical notion that we were made to be in community, and that to flourish as a member of a church you need to be engaged with the people and the church ethos. It would be naive to think that you could divorce yourself from a culture that had a certain set of beliefs and codes, yet claim you're not likely to adopt the dogmas of the next community you join.

I've observed a trend in the North American church. People leave churches that have a clearly stated set of scripturally defined beliefs, because those churches don't exhibit the characteristics that reflect those beliefs. These believers then join other churches that have little in common with what they've stated they believe, but the new place exhibits the missing characteristics of their former congregation. Seemingly without fail, their new culture, with its own moral codes and language, changes this person's fundamental understanding of what it means to be a Christian. In the absence of a Christian community that fosters and strengthens a biblically directed faith, our beliefs will morph into those of the culture around us.

BEING HIS FOLLOWER, ACCORDING TO JESUS

Perhaps the most analyzed text about "discipleship" (developing as a follower of Christ) is "The Great Commission." Subsequent to Jesus's resurrection on Easter Sunday, during an appearance to His followers, He gave them this directive:

> "All authority in heaven and on earth has been given
> to me. Therefore, go and make disciples of all nations,

baptizing them in the name of the Father and of the
Son and of the Holy Spirit, and teaching them to obey
everything I have commanded you. And surely I am with
you always, to the very end of the age."
Matthew 28:18-20

Regarding the necessity for community in order to grow in your faithfulness to following Jesus, here are some reflections from Jesus's famous decree to the church: (1) Discipleship is about following the One who is ruling the world from His throne; (2) Discipleship is carried out by mature Christians leading younger Christians by learning together what Jesus said and did; (3) Discipleship involves learning obedience to what Jesus has commanded; and (4) Discipleship takes place continuously in the presence of Jesus.

For those who don't believe that Jesus rose from His grave in 33 A.D., the notion of Him sitting on a throne in heaven and ruling the world is absurd. Therefore, following and obeying Him seems even more foolish. However, for those who believe that Jesus lives and reigns according to the testimony of the New Testament apostles, following Him is not optional. The alternative is telling the God of the universe, "Thanks, but no." Discipleship is about following the One who is ruling the world from His throne. It is only in light of His deity that Jesus's teachings don't seem like those of a controlling cult leader. For example, our Savior said:

"Anyone who loves their father or mother more than me is
not worthy of me; anyone who loves their son or daughter
more than me is not worthy of me. Whoever does not take
up their cross and follow me is not worthy of me. Whoever
finds their life will lose it, and whoever loses their life for
my sake will find it."
Matthew 10:37-39

Jesus is to be obeyed because He is the Son of God who has existed from before all human time. He is as much God as the Father or the Holy Spirit (they are one in being, three in persons) and is to be worshipped as such. His current position at the right hand of the Father, with all authority in heaven and on earth, is the substantial basis of our being His followers. If Jesus wasn't, by nature, God and the ruler of the universe, He wouldn't deserve to be obeyed.

The great theologian John Owen wrote this about the gospel as it pertains to Christ being substantially one with God for all of eternity:

> "The whole purpose of grace is to glorify the whole Trinity, and the way this is done is by reaching up to the Father's love through the work of the Spirit and the blood of the Son. Divine love begins with the Father, is carried on by the Son and then communicated to us by the Spirit. The Father purposes, the Son purchases, and the Holy Spirit effectively brings it to pass. So, we are brought by the work of the Spirit to faith in the blood of Christ, by which we are accepted by the Father."[11]

It reflects God's character and being when Jesus's followers live in this type of community. Why? Because within the one God of three persons, He has always lived this way.

FOLLOWERS ARE MADE BY OTHER FOLLOWERS

Just as Jesus trained His entourage of twelve to be His followers, Christian discipleship is carried out by mature Christians leading younger Christians. This was the clear command of Jesus when He told the apostles to go and make disciples, teaching them to obey. Learning together is an important part of the discipleship process. We study what Jesus said and did, we discuss and contemplate what that means for our lives, and then encourage each other to imitate His love for God and our neighbors.

When I first became a Christian, I suffered from the lack of a mentor. Then I went to college and had older Christians take me under their care and show me what it meant to follow Jesus. Sure, there was a learning component to it, but as the old adage maintains, "More is caught than taught." By watching believers in my church community, I learned what genuine Christianity was. As I started to grow, my emotions bounced all over the place, and it was confusing. I was super zealous for Jesus as a new believer, but if not for the mentors I had as I grew, I would have been confused by my unexpected struggles. In her terrific book *Extravagant Grace*, Barbara Duguid writes:

> "Baby Christians feel more than they think, and their feelings often depend on how well they are doing in the realm of obedience. The judgmental spirit in which they evaluate others often carries over to the way they evaluate themselves. When they succeed in their religious disciplines, they think that God takes more delight in them than when they fail."[12]

If not for people discipling me through my growth stages, I would've continued making foolish judgments about myself and others. As a follower of Christ, I am led by more mature disciples, and simultaneously I'm a disciple maker of those younger in the faith than I am.

FOLLOWERS LEARN TO OBEY WHAT JESUS SAID

Later in this book, we'll explore how we can have confidence that the New Testament contains Jesus's actual words. The shortest answer is that Jesus told the disciples that the Holy Spirit would enable them to remember all that He'd taught them, and the Spirit would also lead them in developing doctrinal truth for the church.[13] When Jesus commanded the disciples to go, it was not just to collect people for an indiscriminate purpose. Our Lord intended for the process His apostles went through to be experienced by others too. They would meet Jesus by the grace of the Father drawing them, walk with Jesus and see how He lived, and listen to Jesus to hear what He taught was true and right. Christ's disciples experienced the grace that led to good works, and future disciples would do the same. To grow as a believer, you need someone you trust to teach you to obey "all that He commanded."

In his classic book *Celebration of Discipline*, Richard Foster remarked:

> "God does guide the individual richly and profoundly, but He also guides groups of people and can instruct the individual through the group experience. Perhaps our preoccupation with private guidance is the product of our Western individualism. The people of God have not always been so."[14]

FOLLOWERS ENJOY THE PRESENCE OF JESUS

Perhaps no greater assurance from God exists in Scripture than "Never will I leave you; never will I forsake you."[15] For the Christian, this means that the Holy Spirit lives within us. Therefore, it's impossible for us to ever be without God. To the Old Testament people of God, it was understood that God would in His omnipotence (all-powerful), omniscience (all-knowing), and omnipresence (all-everywhere) providentially oversee every step of life. When Jesus says, "I will be with you always," He specifically hints at His forthcoming promise about the work of the Holy Spirit within each believer.[16] What makes this promise so delightful is that knowing God is present leads us to pursue the enjoyment of Him. The Westminster Shorter Catechism, Question #1 asks, "What is the chief end of man?" The answer: "To glorify God and enjoy Him forever."

The enjoyment of Jesus's presence through the Holy Spirit produces love for God. Love for God is the ideal motivation for obedience. It's always good to do what is right, but that doesn't always mean you're doing so out of love for God. In Jesus's time, some religious leaders obeyed Old Testament law but had no real love or affection for God and saw no need to have a relationship with Jesus. They obeyed because they were scared to death of Him. That's true in our time, too, as some people mistakenly confuse compliance with adoration. I can begrudgingly buy flowers for my wife, thinking that my gifts for her are required so she won't leave me. But the "I do this only because I have to" attitude wouldn't bring any joy to her.

In the same way, we love God because we are growing in our comprehension of His love for us, and in our confidence that He's promised He'll never leave us. Growing in grace involves daily appreciation and reflection upon the presence of God's Spirit, made possible by the work of Christ to redeem believers. Meditating on God's presence and the promises of His Word is one of best ways to grow in our faith. But that practice is first taught to us by others (I'd never conceived of a personal devotional time before going to college), which demonstrates (again) the necessity for Christ followers to develop genuine community within their own local church.

NOT SO FREE SOLO

Alex Honnold is the mountain climber who scaled El Capitan without ropes in the Academy Award-winning film *Free Solo*. While the film made clear that Honnold had natural physical and mental abilities that made him stand above the climbing world, *Free Solo* also provided a fascinating behind-the-scenes look at the people in his life. The film showed his unparalleled work ethic, but also included introductions to all those who played critical roles in his success. Initially, free soloing was Alex's escape from the anxiety of relationships. However, when it came time to train for the famous climb up El Capitan, he brought his friend and climbing mentor with him. While he does quite a bit of his training alone, there were relationships in his life that he depended on for emotional support. He needed others in spite of his amazing individual talent.

Many Christians believe they can abandon church community and continue to climb spiritually. That notion contrasts with how Jesus has designed us, as people who grow by constant contact with other believers. His church is a place where iron sharpens iron, older teaches teach younger, and the more experienced assist the less experienced.[17] "Church-free" living may be the path that you are on at the moment, but as a Christian, you need to know that God has not made you to go alone on this Christian journey. Jesus has commanded you to be part of a church family, if for no other reason than to meet others' needs and experience the joy produced by giving. Finally, for your own thriving, He has commanded you to be part of a church that genuinely believes the gospel (there are so-called churches that do not—more about that later in this book).

Tip #1 – Never go alone

Spiritual health thrives in genuine community.

Tip #2: Know your limitations

Spiritual strength develops with
growing humility.

When I moved to Los Angeles from the East Coast, I boasted to my friends back home that I was not all that impressed with celebrities. As a professor of media and culture studies, I'd observed some Hollywood celebrities with public relations issues or a desire to recapture lost fame quickly become spokespeople for a wide variety of causes. From time to time I had seen celebrity publicity stunts which, when combined with a sinful envy of their influence and money, can produce arrogant disdain, for actors in particular. I confess that some of that was cooking in my system. Hence, I proudly saw myself as someone who wouldn't read celebrity magazines, watch *Extra* or *Entertainment Tonight*, or become starstruck.

I live in the Pasadena area of Los Angeles, which is an upscale community that is home to many wealthy and influential people. Actors who live in the area tend not to want to be noticed or bothered. Every so often, one might spot a famous person at a coffee shop or walking along the shops and restaurants of Old Town Pasadena. For the most part, however, A-list celebrities prefer to move about undetected and unbothered by strangers who want to take selfies with them or get their autographs. They generally move into gated communities around the city to prevent stalking or privacy encroachments by the ubiquitous paparazzi. However, they are normal people, in the sense that most have kids who go to school and they like to go to the grocery store, just like I do.

One afternoon I left my office, which is right off the famed Colorado Boulevard, the street which the "The Little Old Lady from Pasadena" sped down in the classic Jan and Dean song. The drugstore that I was headed to was also on that main drag, a four-lane road with a rose-colored line painted down the center—a line that the Rose Bowl Parade floats use as a guide every New Year's Day. I picked up my prescription and was walking out the front door when I found myself face to face with Jack Black, one of my favorite actors. *Nacho Libre* has always been in my top five movies because I am a minister, and that movie has hilariously been a source of encouragement to me in my calling.

So, there was Jack Black in the flesh, along with his young son. What did I do at that moment? I blurted out, "Mr. Jack!" He looked at me oddly (this clearly wasn't his first crazy fan experience) and somewhat reluctantly said, "Hi" and continued walking into the store. Flustered that I couldn't come up with anything better than combining an honorific with his first name, I added (as he walked away), "I love you!"

There are few images I can conjure up that are more embarrassing than a middle-aged man getting starstruck in the entrance of a Rite Aid. I walked back to my car and relearned an important lesson from King Solomon's Proverbs: Pride goes before a fall. I thought I was above the celebrity worshippers of the world. I learned otherwise.

Ironically, to get strong spiritually, Christians must retain an ever-present sense of weakness and humility. Tip #2 of the Three Tips is "Know your limitations." When hiking for the first time, people are warned not to attempt things they're unaccustomed to trying. If you watch enough movies or have seen a few documentaries about rock or mountain climbing, you know that professionals make difficult actions look easy. Amateurs can get hurt trying things they're incapable of achieving. Humility is the key to interacting with our culture, too. One of the church's most visible sins has been its failure to admit mistakes. Elton John's hit sums it up well: "Sorry seems to be the hardest word." It shouldn't be so for churches, but as we'll see in this section of the book, humility doesn't come naturally to human beings. We'll explore how Christians are charged, for their own good, to be humble with each other, our God, and the world around us. I'll address questions that those who have wandered away from church have asked, and I'll show how our choice to be humble (or not) affects us and others.

Chapter 4—The Sin Conundrum: Why do human beings react so strongly against biblical definitions of human brokenness?

Chapter 5—The "Great" BIG Problem: Has the church adopted the culture's definitions of success?

Chapter 6—The Status Struggle: Do Christians really see themselves as equals with the less fortunate?

Sometimes, Jesus's teachings are embraced by friends and family who are not Christians. Who can argue with our Savior's instructions to love our neighbor or sacrifice to help the needy? But when Jesus's teaching and mission are correctly understood to mean that humans are desperately lost and without hope apart from Christ's saving grace, cultural attitudes change quickly. This section of our book will help us embrace who we truly are, something that is possible only if we understand that we're safe before God when we admit our weakness. Genuine community (Tip #1) isn't possible without growing humility.

FOUR.

The Sin Conundrum

I n the Washington, D.C. suburbs where I grew up, many of my classmates had parents with high-profile careers. In 1979, the dad of one of my friends was front and center as the nation was terrified that we were watching a nuclear plant meltdown in Pennsylvania. We were. Of course, as a teenager I had no idea that my friend's dad was a central figure in this national drama. I just knew that he was a nice man.

In the early morning of March 28, 1979, a malfunction in a cooling system valve at the Three Mile Island nuclear plant near Harrisburg, Pennsylvania, brought a region of the country to the brink of an unthinkable disaster. When contaminated water leaked into an adjoining building and released radioactive gas into the plant, Three Mile Island became the storied place where the first official general emergency happened at a U.S. nuclear power plant. A combination of technical failure and human error and misunderstanding created a week of national anxiety. By the time the plant engineers managed to pinpoint the problem and cool off the reactor, over half of the nuclear plant core had melted down.

Two days later, a new fear began to take hold, further shaking an already nervous public. My friend's dad, who was a senior Nuclear Regulatory Engineer and considered the nation's leading expert on emergency core cooling, had determined that a hydrogen gas bubble had formed above the reactor core and was dangerously close to exploding. As panic spread throughout the Eastern Seaboard, other NRC engineers began assessing the likelihood of an explosion. They discovered that the wrong formula was being used to conclude that a hydrogen explosion was imminent. The engineers were able to safely burn off the hydrogen and the community was safe from danger.[1] It's remarkable that the smartest men in the world can make the tiniest of errors, and when the stakes are that high, the results can be life altering for so many.

When you have an important formula, and there is an unaccounted-for or faulty "X" factor, the results will be erroneous. Put even more simply, if the equation 10 + "X" = 15, and you figure "X"

= 8, your answer of 18 is wrong. In a sense, that's what happened at Three Mile Island, with regard to the hydrogen bubble. They made a minor miscalculation that could've produced a terrible result, and they added to an already sky-high anxiety level.

Christianity has an "X" factor that is often omitted when philosophers, scholars, politicians, or armchair theologians assess Christian doctrine and practice. When this "X" factor is removed from the equation or its value is misunderstood, the resulting conclusion is erroneous. The "X" factor here is the catastrophic fall of human beings into what the Bible calls sin. This Christian doctrine contends that "the fall" distorted humanity's ability to see the world correctly. It warped human nature, making it selfish and proud. The fall also had physical ramifications for our universe, and humanity in particular. All manner of human brokenness is considered by theologically orthodox Christians to be by-products of the separation between the Creator and His creation.

Judeo-Christian theology has always taught that as a result of the first human rebellion against God, the world has operated as a beautiful, yet severely broken place. The result of this fracture in the intended condition of our universe is that human beings have been cut off from natural friendship with God, natural moral ability has been stripped from us, and the natural world itself is now full of disruptions that were not part of God's intention for the universe. Theologian J.I. Packer wrote:

> "The truth, however, is that in many respects, and
> certainly in spiritual matters, we are all weak and
> inadequate, and we need to face it. Sin, which disrupts all
> relationships, has disabled us all across the board. We need
> to be aware of our limitations and to let this awareness
> work in us humility and self-distrust, and a realization of
> our helplessness on our own."[2]

The lack of understanding about the effects of humankind's fall from God's gracious presence has rendered a generation of churchgoers unable to explain why "I was born this way" is an unacceptable reason for disobeying biblical commands. One of the purposes of God's commands is to set us on a course to remake our world as it was before the fall. Hence, because of the rebellion of our first parents, a natural disposition to ignore what God's Word says is every human's default position. We're all working against that impairment. We can and should be compassionate with each other in our brokenness, as we are all affected by the fall.

I've learned that some people walk away from the faith because they have a misunderstood "X" factor. Therefore, things don't seem to add up. This miscalculation makes life difficult for the believer to navigate within Western culture, and certainly makes a Scripture-directed life appear out of step with modern society. For instance, without a correct understanding of the biblical description of the fall, Christians appear to be small-minded and unenlightened for concluding that people should not automatically trust their natural inclinations. One may disagree with Christian theology about human nature, but they shouldn't assign ill motives or hatred to people who honestly believe that this is how the Scriptures describe the world.

If you follow Christ, whose Word gives directives to correct the problems in our world and in our relationships, you have little choice but to trust and obey Him. Christians have held this understanding about humanity's sin and brokenness from time immemorial, long before the 21st-century culture wars of the West. For Christians, the Old and New Testaments serve as corrective lenses for human beings whose ability to see the world was distorted from birth. According to Scripture, humanity's perception of reality is inaccurate. If a person who identifies as a Christian doesn't believe this, that is the "X" factor that will logically alter the way the world looks to them.

This chapter will explore how our lack of humility before God can negatively affect our growth as Christians. We've already discussed (in part) the sociological phenomenon of human pride and how that keeps people from believing that they need community. We'll also explore the rational, biblical, and theological reasons for belief in the fall. And we'll contemplate how this should prevent Christians from developing an attitude that communicates, "I can do this without God." Most would never say this aloud, but our actions and/or inaction can reveal how we really think and feel.

WHO DENIES THAT EVIL EXISTS?

Evil exists. Only the deluded deny it. The Nazi Party in Germany oversaw the extermination of an estimated several million Jews in their concentration camps. Lest we forget, WWII also needlessly took the lives of tens of millions of soldiers and civilians from multiple countries. Driving this mass destruction of human life were the evil impulses of a German fascist with a goal of world domination. Aside from the atrocities of the First and Second World Wars (both instigated by Germany), in the second half of the twentieth century, the communist government of East Germany had allied itself with the Soviet Union. The communists also had aspirations of world domination. It was a tough 20th century for the Deutschland.

Hitler and other dictators are the most obvious evidences of evil in the world. Evil is not simply the "really bad" actions that people do. The Christianity of Scripture maintains that all human beings possess a sinful nature that, when unleashed, is the opposite of God's character. God's commands are presented in Scripture as reflections of His attributes and character. For instance, God is a creator of human beings. To take human life by murder is to act in opposition to God's character. This is why the fifth of the Ten Commandments is "Thou shalt not murder." To be controlled by evil is to say that one cannot help but do what is wrong and harmful to others. Criminal sociopathology is often the explanation for serial killers' and contract assassins' actions. These coldhearted murderers have no natural capacity for empathy. We characterize this type of detached immorality as evil. But all human beings are capable of evil to varying degrees, because of the nature they possess due to the fall.

That said, in this sinful and broken world, we followers of Jesus have been taught to pray that our Heavenly Father would not lead us into temptation but deliver us from evil.[3] Because of the fall, we are the potential proponents of evil actions, either actively or passively. Indeed, most human beings agree that people can do evil. Christians maintain that the existence of sin and evil is a result of humanity's fall from God's presence and the resulting judgment of our first parents' actions. One direct result of their rebellion against the Creator was the passing on of their sinful nature to us. This nature renders us incapable of moral good apart from God's grace. The grace to do good comes to human beings in various forms (i.e., societal laws, cultural standards, or family moral influence), but without those restraints, human nature will put the individual first at the expense of everyone, including God.

I recognize this rebellious nature in myself when it comes to obeying the speed limit. Perhaps I'm not alone in confessing this, but when I'm certain that law enforcement isn't watching or that every other vehicle on the highway is exceeding the posted speed limit, I will put the pedal to the metal. Since I was a child, I've realized this tendency to disobey if I can get away with it. Most parents would testify to seeing this in their own beloved little angels too.

According to theologian Charles Hodge, rebellion existed in the world before the creation of humans. Satan and his angels were cast from heaven. In the same way, humans were cast from God's presence when Adam sinned. However, creation, as God originally spoke it into existence, was free from shame, pain, suffering, and death.[4] This was all interrupted when human beings committed an act that the late theologian R.C. Sproul described as "cosmic treason."[5]

The scene of human rebellion was set in the Garden of Eden, where in unity with God, Adam and Eve were given complete freedom and rule over the new creation. There was only one stipulation to their stewardship of God's world: They were not to eat of the Tree of the Knowledge of Good and Evil. They did. Instantaneously, they realized that they were naked, and they were ashamed. Without having to pronounce them guilty, their sin had already negatively affected their existence. When God spoke to them, He issued the following judgments and consequences for their disobedience to His commands:

> To the woman he said, "I will make your pains in childbearing very severe; with painful labor you will give birth to children. Your desire will be for your husband, and he will rule over you." To Adam he said, "Because you listened to your wife and ate fruit from the tree about which I commanded you, 'You must not eat from it,' cursed is the ground because of you; through painful toil you will eat food from it all the days of your life. It will produce thorns and thistles for you, and you will eat the plants of the field. By the sweat of your brow you will eat your food until you return to the ground, since from it you were taken; for dust you are and to dust you will return."
> **Genesis 3:16-19**

The fall resulted in three changes that were not part of God's intention for His holy creation. Incidentally, Jesus has promised that at the consummation of human history, He will eradicate sin and its effects on God's creation. The three results of the fall were:

1) Disruption in the physical universe. The ground wouldn't easily produce the food they needed to survive. We can also derive from this that the broken world then produced famines and other natural disasters.

2) Difficulty in the process of giving birth. Before the fall, children would be born without pain or flaw. Subsequent to the sin of our first parents, childbirth would be excruciatingly difficult and dangerous.

3) Destruction of human relationships, brought on by human

selfishness. This would first be evidenced by Eve's experiencing her husband's natural sinful compulsion to rule her (as opposed to the servant leader model Jesus spoke of in Mark 10:42-45).

Throughout history, humanity has continually seen this evil instinct to selfishly dominate others through human and economic exploitation. Men have taken advantage of their biological strength advantage and subjugated women. Human beings have enslaved other human beings for their own benefit. Stronger, geographically bigger, and more affluent nations have sought conquest over smaller, poorer, and economically vulnerable countries. There is only one word that adequately characterizes how Scripture describes the effects of humanity's fall from God's gracious presence: catastrophic. On every imaginable level.

Evil exists in our world. Only the delusional deny it.

GOD AND SIN

A student from the local seminary once asked me why God was so uptight with Adam and Eve. They wanted to know why the consequences of human sin were so severe. I responded by saying that God seems overly reactive about human sin only from our perspective. We tend to portray our own sin as inconsequential, while being overly offended by the sins of others. As my siblings and I used to say, "Skunks can't smell their own P.U." We also fail to assess our own sins accurately, usually omitting sinful attitudes (like pride, which is offensive to Jesus) or sins of omission (the things we could've done but didn't care enough). In our own eyes, human beings often seem fairly close to being good people. It's not uncommon to hear someone contend, "No one's perfect, but we're basically good people." In light of our natural tendency to overrate ourselves, it makes sense that people would imagine that the God of the Bible was a bit severe.

To demonstrate why God's holiness cannot tolerate even a little of our sin (presuming arrogantly that we have only a little), I will conduct a little experiment. I offer someone a brand-new, unopened bottle of spring water. Once they respond affirmatively that they would like it, I unscrew the cap and put my mouth on the opening. Not only that, I drop a small bit of my saliva into the bottle, put the cap back on and then shake it up. My spit then constitutes an infinitesimal amount of the total liquid in the bottle. However, unless they have just concluded a walk across California's Mojave Desert, they all reject my offer to drink from the barely tainted bottle of water. Now, multiply the level of pollution in that bottle by a large factor, and you'll see how repulsive sin is to a perfect and holy God. We think our sin is just a drop. In reality, it's an ocean.

From God's perspective, our collective disobedience is also offensive because it does more than violate His moral law. It's a personal transgression of distrust against Him. Sproul said, "Sin is not restricted merely to an external action that transgresses a divine law. Rather, it represents an internal motive, a motive that is driven by an inherent hostility toward the God of the universe."[6] In practical terms, a perfect being cannot be touched by the presence of one speck of evil or that being wouldn't be perfectly holy any longer. Holiness is the complete absence of sin, so sinful beings were cut off from God's presence. As we'll see in Chapter Seven, God, through Jesus, solved the dilemma of requiring purity in His presence and His separation from a morally bent people whom He loved.

The Scriptures teach we're rebellious toward God's laws from birth.[7] All of us are in the same boat, having been born with varying natural proclivities to disobey God's Word.[8] The purpose of God's redemptive plan in Christ is to restore human beings to fellowship with their Creator and restore God's glory in His creation. This is done when Jesus's followers resist our human nature and exhibit the new nature we have in Christ. Ultimately, God's creation intentions will be restored, and His children will live forever, without disordered desires or natural inclinations to do anything out of step with their Father's perfect being. This salvation from our deeds and our nature will happen because Jesus has taken the place of all who believe. He became the scapegoat for our sins.

The New Testament letter to the Romans says:

> "There is no difference between Jew and Gentile, for all
> have sinned and fall short of the glory of God, and all are
> justified freely by his grace through the redemption that
> came by Christ Jesus. God presented Christ as a sacrifice
> of atonement, through the shedding of his blood—to be
> received by faith."
> **Romans 3:22b-25a**

Verse 23 says we've not just fallen short of perfection ... we're not even close. We're given to saying things like "No one's perfect," but that's usually to make ourselves feel better when we feel bad about doing something awful to someone. The above text states that there is no difference among any of us, because we all have sinned and "fallen short." The metaphor here is one that was used in ancient archery. The glory of God is the center of the target. Not only did we miss the bull's-eye, we fell considerably short of the whole target.

Verses 24 and 25 demonstrate the severity of our sin problem and provide one more reason why theologically orthodox Christians contend that the fall was disastrous: If the gulf between our Heavenly Father and us was fixable by human effort, why did Jesus, the Son of God, have to die on a cross? If our foibles were not at all offensive to God and don't deserve His just displeasure and judgment, why did a man from Galilee suffer so greatly and (apparently) unnecessarily? Where was a just God when the completely innocent Jesus of Nazareth was tortured to death? How does a benevolent Deity do nothing while this kind of evil runs rampant on the innocent?

WHERE IS GOD WHEN EVIL HAPPENS?

Philosophers have long argued that the presence of evil means that God doesn't exist, or He does but is unable to stop evil. Judeo-Christian theology claims God does have the power to stop it and will, eventually. We contend that in this interim season between the fall and the final judgment of humanity, God remains sovereign over evil, using it to accomplish His purposes. Philosopher Alvin Plantinga characterized Saint Augustine's answer to this problem:

> "Augustine tries to tell us what God's reason is for permitting evil. At bottom, he says, it's that God can create a more perfect universe by permitting evil. A really top-notch universe requires the existence of free, rational, and moral agents; and some of the free creatures He created went wrong. But the universe with the free creatures it contains and the evil they commit is better than it would have been had it contained neither the free creatures nor this evil."[9]

In Scripture we see that sometimes God actively opposes evil; at other times He passively allows it. In either case, God's providential benevolence enables Him to take that which was meant for evil and use it for good.[10] To reinforce this idea, one need look no further than the life and death of Jesus Christ. Scripture maintains that God actively initiated a rescue plan to remedy the sin conundrum into which humanity placed itself. God's plan of action solved the obvious and primary result of evil, the separation of individual human beings from personal relationship with their Creator. Through this restoration of fellowship through Jesus Christ, God now often actively opposes evil through those who are genuinely His children.

On the other side of the coin, the idea that God passively allows evil to bring about the good is also evidenced in Jesus's death. Since its inception, the Christian church has maintained that for our salvation, Jesus came down from heaven. The Father's redemption plan was for His innocent Son to willingly exchange His life for all who would ever put their trust in His free gift of forgiveness. Jesus of Nazareth would suffer an unjust death so that those who receive Him as Savior would have their sins atoned for through His sacrifice. He was the "Lamb of God, who takes away the sin of the world!"[11]

Jesus simultaneously satisfies the justice of a God who cannot ignore evil, and also forgives the humble sinner who calls out to Him for mercy. This part of God's redemptive plan required His passive allowance for evil. Scripture tells us that Jesus was falsely accused, tried, and found guilty in a kangaroo court. The mob on Good Friday refused to cry out to Pontius Pilate for clemency on Jesus's behalf, instead encouraging the release of a murderer. Then, sadistic Roman soldiers beat Jesus to near unconsciousness, flayed His skin with a lead-tipped whip called a flagrum, and made Him walk the humiliating journey to the hill called Golgotha. There the Roman soldiers drove spikes into His hands and feet and mocked Him while He suffered. Jesus died by suffocation on a cross built for the worst of sinners, like me. He died in front of His mom and one of His best friends. God allowed that evil for us and our salvation.

In step with Augustine, we can conclude the reason God passively allowed such evil was to glorify His Son Jesus and bring about good. Christ's heroic sacrifice has led to the salvation of an untold number of souls. These children of God had been anticipating the Messiah's arrival for centuries before Jesus. More children of God over the two millennia since Jesus's death have looked back to His sacrifice, called out for mercy, and received unconditional grace and love. Jesus was resurrected from His borrowed tomb, and, according to the Scriptures, ascended into heaven, where He is seated at the right hand of God the Father. The Nicene Creed declares that Jesus will come again in glory to judge the living and the dead.[12] None of this happens if Jesus isn't unjustly dealt with by evil human beings influenced by other evil men. And Jesus trusted in His Father's sovereignty.

"For the joy set before him he endured the cross, scorning its shame, and sat down at the right hand of the throne of God."
Hebrews 12:2

HUMILITY BEFORE GOD

Aside from offending our gracious God and Father, how would the lack of humility before God negatively affect our life? First, there is an ever-present possibility that we are not seeing and hearing things accurately. We may be foolish enough to presume we're right when we're wrong. Not being able to admit we're wrong (because we refuse to see or can't see) makes relationships a challenge. Humility is needed for personal and corporate relationship reconciliation. If I'm not willing to admit my culpability in the fracturing of a relationship, there is little chance of that relationship being restored.

Christianity has always been naturally difficult for people to embrace because it requires humility before God. A person cannot become a Christian unless they bow before Jesus, the King of the universe. They must confess their offenses to Him and then receive the grace and mercy He has provided through His death as our substitute. Our pride keeps us from admitting our need for a pardon from God. Like the prisoner who can't face up to his crimes and continues to delude himself into thinking he's innocent, our nature bucks the idea of bowing before anyone or begging for clemency.

Our success-driven culture fuels the sense that kneeling before another is the lowest thing one could do. In Frank Sinatra's signature anthem, "My Way," he boastfully sang of his successful domination of the challenges that he alone has faced, and his refusal to kneel. The entire tune could be the theme song for delusional Western individualism, which is why Sinatra's daughter says he actually hated the song and found it self-indulgent. But his fan base loved it, so he had to keep performing.[13]

GQ Magazine's Scott Meslow wrote that the song pays tribute to "a deeply obnoxious philosophy: the idea that the purest way for a man to live his life is to constantly push forward without ever questioning his own methods or allowing any criticism, right or wrong, to penetrate his thick skull."[14] Individualistic pride about how we've done it our way, and how we won't kneel before anyone, is antithetical to being a Christian. If you want to follow the man from

Galilee, then like a child you're going to have put your hand in the hand of the man who stilled the waters and calmed the sea. And he's told us to humble ourselves before one another.

Kneeling before God is an act of humility,

"You don't have to kneel before God to be humble before Him or to pray. But you do have to pray in order to be humble before God. Prayer is how the Christian gets in tune with God."

and that's why prayer is so often depicted as being done this way. You don't have to kneel before God to be humble before Him or to pray. But you do have to pray in order to be humble before God. Prayer is how the Christian gets in tune with God. Prayer is how the follower of Christ reminds herself that apart from Jesus, she can do nothing.[15] Prayer is how we specifically ask God for the power to live as He has commanded, and it is the only means by which this supernatural strength is appropriated.[16]

We can tell a lot about how truly dependent we are on God by how frequently we pray. Oh, we love to say things like "I know I can do nothing without Jesus," but so often we don't act like we believe it. I can attest to the fact that if there is no genuine communication going on between me and my Creator, it is usually because I don't think I need Him bad enough. If I'm in a real pinch and know I need God's supernatural power, I will quickly make room for prayer.

HUMILITY HELPS US

A second way that humility before God benefits us is how it produces healthier relationships with other people. Proud people tend to be difficult to deal with. Who hasn't had a supervisor who thought too much of themselves, or a spouse who was unrelenting in their demands? People who are perfectionists often act this way to earn the praise they crave, and they enforce their "high standards" not for the benefit of those around them, but out of fear that they might look bad.

Hypocrisy also is a feature of the arrogant person, and their words betray how foolish they are. I chuckle when I hear people declare things like, "I hate people who don't love their fellow man" or "Do not tolerate the intolerant." Proud people often don't recognize the contradictory propositions contained in their own declarations.

Again, prayer serves us well here because when someone can even briefly conceive of God's magnitude and magnificence, they will find it proportionally difficult to be a jerk to others. When you recognize, through prayer and meditation on God's Word, that He has been supremely patient with a sinner like you, it should translate into an increased level of compassion for others who are just like you. Once we realize how much we have been forgiven by a perfect, Holy God, it is the zenith of foolishness to withhold forgiveness from others who are no more sinful than we are. Only by fathoming our own sins against a Holy God (which spring from our bent and broken nature) can we reflect His graciousness to others. We can't love our neighbor as we love ourselves if we don't love ourselves as God does. This is what walking humbly with our God does. Through prayer we practice forgiveness for others by praying for those who have mistreated us.[17]

DAZED DRIVING

A few years back, I traveled from California to speak at a Christian high school in Orlando. To save money, I took a red-eye flight that left at 12:30 a.m., Pacific time, and landed in Orlando at 8:30 a.m., Eastern time. I rushed from the airport to the school, spoke at 11:00 a.m., and then had lunch with a friend until 1:30 p.m. From there I drove my rental car northwest to see friends in Ocala and Gainesville. I arrived at one friend's house in Gainesville at 5:00 p.m., had dinner and hung out there until 8:00 p.m. I still had another hour and a half to drive to get to another friend's river house in Yankeetown. Here was the problem: In all of the excitement of seeing friends and speaking at a school, I had not realized how long it had been since I slept. By the time I got to the last 90-minute leg of my journey, I had been awake since 7 the previous morning. That's just over 36 hours without rest. Funny thing was, I didn't feel tired.

From Gainesville I took the two-lane State Highway 24 west toward my final destination on the Gulf of Mexico. This part of central Florida is pretty remote and doesn't have an abundance of street or highway lighting. I drove without incident on the first highway and then made a left turn, heading south onto State Highway 98, the main highway going into Citrus County. The intersection of 24 and 98 was really dark, but there were no cars coming from either direction, so pulling onto another two-lane highway was done without incident.

Not long after I turned south, I began to notice a couple of strange things. First, the reflectors in the middle of the highway were red. That was the first time I'd seen that, and I figured because there was so much rain in Florida, they chose a color that would grab your attention while driving in a deluge. Not long after that, I noticed that the cars on this two-lane highway were driving awfully recklessly. They were passing cars in front of me and then just barely pulling back into their lane as I approached. A third oddity kept occurring, as well. Cars to my right on the access road were traveling as fast as I was. While I was accustomed to side roads adjacent to a highway, it was unusual for those cars to travel faster than the ones on the highway.

Then it dawned on me. I wasn't on a two-lane highway. I was on a four-lane highway with a median, and I was headed dangerously southbound into northbound traffic. To my right, people in cars were hanging out of their windows trying to get my attention. And those red reflectors? Those are to warn you that you're on the wrong side of the highway. I quickly found a break in the median and got to the correct side of the road, but now I had cars following me closely. They were writing down my license plate number and calling the state police, figuring I was a drunk driver. When the police eventually pulled me over, I explained to them that I was following phone directions (which didn't specify a four-lane road), it was dark at the intersection where I turned onto the highway, and that I hadn't been

> " We need His power to follow Jesus, and His grace to trust Him with all of our hearts. Spiritual strength develops with growing humility."

drinking but rather hadn't slept in a day-and-a-half.

Remarkably, even though I could've killed someone (including myself), they let me off with a warning. That's the only time I've been badly impaired by lack of sleep. To my shame, I can tell you that as a youngster I was impaired by other things, but in this case the disability was caused by something I needed but didn't give myself: sleep. Not sleeping enough was poor judgment on my part, but it wasn't something I did knowing that I was endangering others. I was innocently unaware of how incapable I was of seeing things correctly. I felt fine, and the police sobriety examination wouldn't have revealed anything out of the ordinary. However, I couldn't comprehend the circumstances accurately. As a result, I put many lives in danger.

The same can be said of my reckless youth, and, I confess, my adult life as well. Too many times, I have followed my foolish impulses and seemingly clear thought processes without much regard for how my actions would affect others or me. By nature, I'm selfish and proud. The Scriptures say this is true of all human beings. Failing to recognize that we're not seeing things clearly is a costly mistake. Humble Christians recognize their need for the corrective vision the Lord offers in a relationship with Him, a relationship that renews our minds. We need His power to follow Jesus, and His grace to trust Him with all of our hearts. Spiritual strength develops with growing humility.

"Trust in the Lord with all your heart and lean not on your own understanding; in all your ways submit to him, and he will make your paths straight. Do not be wise in your own eyes; fear the Lord and shun evil. This will bring health to your body and nourishment to your bones."
Proverbs 3:5-8

FIVE.

The "Great" BIG Problem

Backhanded compliments are funny—when they're not directed at you. A childhood friend who is a Christian reconnected with me through social media, and when she discovered I was a minister, she remarked, "I guess God can use anyone." This is true, but it hit a nerve. I recognize that much of my childhood behavior would not serve as a predictor of future Christian service. More importantly, I humbly recognize I wouldn't be in this vocation if the Lord hadn't graciously worked to bring me to faith. Further, while I have some God-given gifts, they wouldn't work without my Heavenly Father helping people come to faith.[1] My friend was right; God can use *anyone*. I would've preferred a different response from her, but those words humbled me. Again.

If someone says they have great humility, that is a contradiction in terms akin to "jumbo shrimp," "random order," or "act naturally." The only way great humility is not an oxymoron is if you define greatness differently. To be great often connotes superiority. Thinking of oneself as having superior humility would be contradictory. But if greatness is defined as what Jesus has done, as being the servant of all, then growing humility would mean a person is increasingly demonstrating humility by always putting himself in the lower place of serving others. Author Dan Allender wrote:

> "Here is God's leadership model: he chooses fools to live
> foolishly in order to reveal the economy of heaven, which
> reverses and inverts the wisdom of this world. He calls
> us to brokenness, not performance; to relationships, not
> commotion; to grace, not success."[2]

While claims of the American church's acquiescence to Western consumer culture are not new, there is one reason for my asserting anew that we have what I call a "Great" BIG problem (how we've misdefined great and have an unhealthy fascination with large). Our unbiblical definitions of the word "great" and the calibration of success to our world's top prize of being BIG negatively

"
Our 'Great' BIG problem is that we've let our world, our flesh, and the devil define 'great' differently and attract us to BIG instead of biblical."

affects the average person's understanding of the Christian life. A distorted pastoral culture trickles down to the people of the church, who feel they have to wield influence to be valued. For many pastors, the pursuit of Christian celebrity has prioritized image over integrity. In his piece titled "The sad irony of celebrity pastors," Ben Sixsmith wrote, "Making yourself a very public representative of God, rather than a humble messenger, is a dangerous business when you are — like all of us — a very flawed human being." [3]

What is the by-product of the Western church ethos, where leaders of big ministries, big influence, and big budgets shield their assets and their brand at the expense of individual and corporate transparency? The church is given a false impression that size matters more than substance. Back in the 1970s, Francis Schaeffer wrote about this condition. It has undoubtedly gotten worse:

> "We all tend to emphasize big works and big places, but all such emphasis is of the flesh. To think in such terms is simply to hearken back to the old, unconverted, egoist, self-centered Me. This attitude, taken from the world, is more dangerous to the Christian than fleshly amusement or practice." [4]

To protect their great status, Christian leaders pose as gurus while disguising the same deep inner struggle that we all face. Their charade communicates that they have ascended to a level of spirituality that they haven't reached. Use whatever term you want to describe it, but the Bible calls inauthenticity "bearing false witness." Lying. This is why Scripture says we cannot thrive spiritually unless we have growing humility. The apostle Peter taught that we're to humble ourselves before God so that He will lift us up.[5] Christian leaders are not called to promote their success but instead boast in their weakness so that Christ's power may rest on them. This is the telltale sign of Christian maturity. As theologian J.I. Packer wrote:

> "For all Christians, the likelihood is rather that as our discipleship continues, God will make us increasingly weakness-conscious and pain-aware, so that we may learn with Paul that when we are conscious of being weak, then—and only then—may we become truly strong in the Lord. And should we want it any other way?"[6]

Churches where pastors are not authentically humble exhibit one of two characteristics: despair or legalism. Despair comes when people are face to face with the reality that they'll never reach the sacred summit where their pastors claim to live. Legalism is the result of people who haven't accepted the impossibility of reaching this feigned spiritual height. (And strict adherence to whatever the pastor has said is the yardstick used to judge themselves and others.) When it comes full circle and the pastor's deception (passive though it may be) is finally exposed, it does further damage to the church and its reputation.

Because Christian leaders self-protectively hide the truth of how sinful they are, those who follow them don't feel the freedom to confess their sins to one another. Author Rachel Gilson wrote: "I've talked to several women who are embarrassed to discuss the strength of their sexual urges, because it feels like good Christians just shouldn't struggle with that. In each of these scenarios, people

> "**Because Christian leaders self-protectively hide the truth of how sinful they are, those who follow them don't feel the freedom to confess their sins to one another.**"

build walls of silence to protect themselves. But these walls slowly transfigure into prisons."[7]

While it may seem easy to fault the Western church for its mirroring of success culture, this over-fascination with the value of church leadership has been a problem since the church's inception:

> "You are still worldly. For since there is jealousy and quarreling among you, are you not worldly? Are you not acting like mere humans? For when one says, 'I follow Paul,' and another, 'I follow Apollos,' are you not mere human beings? What, after all, is Apollos? And what is Paul? Only servants, through whom you came to believe— as the Lord has assigned to each his task. I planted the seed, Apollos watered it, but God has been making it grow. So neither the one who plants nor the one who waters is anything, but only God, who makes things grow."
> **1 Corinthians 3:3-7**

Christian leaders are nothing compared to God. Paul would add, "Neither is *anything*." But Christian leaders of the orthodox and evangelical Christian sort have spent a lot of energy telling us that "leaders matter." Hundreds of books and internet blog posts are written about how "God uses gifted people." While God does use people according to the gifts He has given them, He also uses marginally gifted people in miraculous ways. Yes, God uses people with limited gifts (see Moses).

From the New Testament's perspective, we are all used in spite of ourselves. However, we are no different than the Israelites of old. We want a king like the nations around us. It is unthinkable that we would follow a leader who isn't a gifted speaker or a John Maxwell leadership disciple. When our current leaders anoint a new leader, we need not know their character. We instinctively (and sometimes foolishly) trust another successful leader's endorsement. Again and again we've seen this practice bring disaster.

In 1990, Jerry Falwell Sr. introduced the televangelism world to the ministry of a 29-year-old minister named Darrell Gilyard (who was mentored by other superstar Baptist leaders). Gilyard's story of growing up under a bridge and then rising to the top tier of Baptist evangelicalism made him one of the up-and-coming young celebrities of that era. Within one year of the Falwell-backed coronation, the story of this new young "prince of preachers" was revealed as fraudulent. Furthermore, he was discovered to have had multiple extramarital affairs. Even after confessing to these massive deceptions, Gilyard was hired by a church where he served for a few years, until he was arrested on charges of lewd and lascivious conduct. He pled guilty, was sentenced, and was registered as a sex offender. He spent four years in jail. Then he was hired again. Why? He was gifted.

I wish I could tell you this was a unique moment in recent history, but that would be far from the truth. Many examples exist, and they will continue happening unless the Western church recalibrates her understanding of "great." I, too, am part of the problem. Whenever I consider whether an online article is worth reading or a conference is worth attending--based solely on the person's known impact--I'm culpable. I was reborn spiritually into this subculture as a young adult, and it has taken a quarter century of ministry for me to recognize my complicity in its systemic failure. As long as we say, "That's just the way it is," nothing will change. But admitting there is a problem is an important first step. Psychologist and seminary professor Chuck DeGroat issued this important declaration:

> "Grandiose systems often resist change, however. They resist because grandiosity works. Integrity gives way to pragmatism; honesty gives way to illusion. The status quo is much easier than the work of becoming self-aware, evaluation, naming reality, letting go, grieving losses, and embracing new pathways. Add to this the toxic groupthink that resists divergent voices or conflicting

visions and you have a recipe for a resistant and
perpetually septic system."[8]

Our "Great" BIG problem drastically redefines what we aim for in our churches and personal spiritual development. We risk missing character-development opportunities in our effort to make a BIG splash of success. Evangelicalism has succumbed to the temptation of prominence, and the consequences are dire. We have fallen for a lie. Our "Great" BIG problem is that we've let our world, our flesh, and the devil define "great" differently and attract us to BIG instead of biblical. When the church allows our world to define greatness, choices are made to protect that status. Scandalous behavior in churches is often hidden to protect the reputation of the church or its leaders. Entire denominations and individual churches have attempted to avoid responsibility and embarrassment by covering up the abuse of children, women, and men. The attempted cover-ups and insufficient sympathy for victims have been as damaging in the public eye as the abuse itself.

The New Testament doesn't teach us to protect the church's reputation, but instead to bring it into the light and expose it. This humble action sets the right example, showing that the church has confidence in God's grace. Paul's first letter to the Corinthians declares that the church has no business judging those outside the church (today it has the reputation of doing that very well). Instead, we're to expose religious scandals without fearing what outsiders think. I can testify to how these worldly emphases on status and size create a context for people with disordered motivations to be drawn into church leadership.

Regardless of the motives for entering into ministry, the pull of potential affirmation and "bigness" can distort one's heart for reaching others. No minister can blame others for their own twisted motivations, as we have to take responsibility for our part. But the American church, and more specifically those in church leadership, must own some responsibility for enabling a culture of celebrity to masquerade as courageous or godly leadership. The unbiblical cultural definition of great and the average church attendee's fascination with "big" success sets the longing soul on a perilous journey of wanting to be a religious star. The "Great" BIG problem of the church is enabling these types. I know because I am one of these ministers.

THE CRASH OF 2008

The film *The Big Short* showed how the 2008 economic crash was largely the fault of the securities-backed mortgage business. Fraudulent credit reports enabled financially unqualified home buyers to get loans from banks. Banks, in turn, bundled those risky loans and sold them to Wall Street. When a massive number of the home loans were defaulted on because the borrowers couldn't afford the higher payment that came with an automatically adjusted rate, the entire industry crumbled. This collapse of securities-backed mortgages caused the failure of several financial institutions and sent shock waves across the financial markets and the international economy. The entire fiscal disaster was the by-product of a false premise and foolish hopes. About that time, a crisis was brewing in my life. It, too, was the result of faulty personal building blocks and a system that fostered my continued foolishness.

At the community relationship level, our "Great" BIG problem keeps us from being real with one another, because we want others to think we are a big deal. It would be hypocritical to call others (including pastors) to a life of humility and openness based on our confidence in the gospel's grace if we're not willing to do the same. I share the following narrative because I believe the Lord wants me to. I contend that the gospel of Jesus Christ frees us to admit sin and to look deep into our hearts to see if there is any offensive way in us. Our internal struggles and life traumas often push ungodly behavior to the surface. Being humble with each other allows us to get beneath the surface to discover our motivations. Sharing these struggles with each other is one way that God transforms us. Hence, the New Testament tells us to confess our sins to each other and pray for each other so that we may be healed.[9]

In the winter of 2008, I was teetering on the brink of a nervous breakdown. After seminary, I began to minister in my hometown of Tallahassee, Florida. As the size and scope of the ministries I was part of grew, so did my need for affirmation and recognition. This unquenchable thirst was not satisfied, because I was too busy (and too "successful") to properly seek affirmation from the Lord. Others tried to warn me of this temptation, and I read books like *Liberating Ministry from the Success Syndrome* by R. Kent Hughes. But when an addict is informally confronted about their problem, they feign agreement, without any real intention of looking inward or ceasing their pursuit of the drug.

My drug was the compulsive need for affirmation, the need to be seen as valuable in comparison to others. Not to get too therapeutic, but years of counseling have helped me see that this unmet need for attention existed in my childhood and was the driving force behind much of my foolish acting out. Many of my teachers from K-12 battled to alter my classroom behavior. As a former disc jockey, I put the struggle into the terms of competing with my teachers for "audience share." As a class clown and entertainer, I saw the classroom as my audience. My exasperated teachers felt differently. Ironically, my father was the president of the national teacher's union, and I was in school making teachers miserable.

It wasn't just the classroom where I was obsessively measuring how I compared to others; being part of the in crowd was the dominant desire in my heart. Unbeknownst to my parents, after we moved to the Washington, D.C. suburbs, I was bullied in elementary school for being an emotionally sensitive boy. Middle school was a welcome fresh start for me. I was a good athlete and not unattractive, so the new culture, composed mostly of people who didn't know me, gave me a new opportunity to redefine myself. I clearly remember sitting in the laundry room of one of the "cool kids" houses. This guy and a few of his cool friends were talking about girls and school, when one of them said, "You're cool, Chuck. You're friends with us." That was what my broken soul was craving to hear.

The trend of measuring myself against the others in the room continued unabated through high school, college, and into my professional career. In college I was exposed to Christian conferences and megachurches where larger-than-life speakers addressed huge crowds. In these early contexts, I began to fill my hunger for affirmation via my new Christian-world experience. Watching the praise that traveling evangelists got from pastors and attendees made me desire to be one.

Subconsciously, I raced after ministry success as a means of feeling important. I founded an organization that put a Christian radio station on the air, pioneered a youth and college ministry, and planted a center-city church. People usually liked me, but I didn't like myself much. I was ashamed of the frightened little kid who was living inside, and my busyness and career ascension were helping cover that up. My need for affirmation was driving me to race my internal engine at an unhealthy level. Perhaps you've noticed on your car's tachometer (which tells the RPM/revolutions per minute) that there is a red area, usually above 8,000 RPM. This is to warn you that when your needle gets into the red, you're in danger of blowing up your engine due to the stress you're placing on it.

During these years of ambition-driven ministry, rarely did anyone ask if I was enjoying the quiet presence of Jesus to refuel my soul. Wherever I was working, we seemed to be winning the ministry race statistically, so any flaws in my character were dealt with only when they became too obvious to ignore. When you run your engine "in the red" while blaring your stereo at eleven, you can't hear much. You can't hear people telling you that you're harming them. You can't hear your children tell you that you're neglecting them. Most of all, you can't hear your own engine, which is clanking, clunking, and on the verge of collapse. But you're having too much fun and getting too much attention to consider that something isn't right.

In 2008 I arrived in California at the small church I was called to pastor into missional success. I immediately began to see and hear troubling signs in myself, including how I was reacting to some challenging situations. I was not succeeding as before, and I started experiencing something that I rarely received in Florida: criticism. I shouldn't have blamed people for this. They had no basis for trusting me, so they questioned what I was doing, in ways I was unaccustomed to being questioned. My friends in Florida always presumed I knew what I was doing and trusted me.

As the criticism mounted and the power families began to exert pressure, I reached a tipping point in my emotional collapse. For the next two months, I had insomnia. When you don't sleep because you're anxious, your ability to process your emotions goes into free fall. Within two months I had to resign, which ultimately resulted in the church's closing its doors. I grieve for my contribution to that process, for I made mistakes. Not the least of these was being out of touch with my soul. Those people needed what I was unable to give them. Unfortunately, I didn't know that at the time.

When your driving force is the admiration of people and you fail to get that affirmation, you have a crisis on your hands. When others' approval gives you life and those who loved you suddenly disapprove of you, it feels like death. I've since learned that my experience is not unique. Fortunately for me, the implosion didn't result in the end of my marriage, or suicide.

MAKE CHRISTIANITY GREAT AGAIN

Reality television and social media have created a new paradigm for success and fame. Formerly, you were famous for being great at something. Now, some are considered great for just being famous. There may not be another city in America so focused on this as Los Angeles, the entertainment capital of the world. As a pastor in Southern California, I can testify that people come here to pursue their dreams. Our church has included aspiring actors, producers, directors, set designers, key grips, and entertainment roles that I never knew existed. Most never achieve "greatness" by the world's standards, but they love their work.

Even when folks reach a level considered successful by industry standards, they often feel that their accomplishments are not enough. If the original goal was to become a full-time working actor, once they achieved that stage, they immediately began to feel the internal pressure to become a "starring actor." What was an accomplishment is now seen as a FAIL. According to a family friend who is an Emmy Award-winning actor, fame is paradoxically a lonely place. The one who longs for fame imagines that being known by the masses will make them feel a greater sense of love. However, the masses don't really know you. Often, they just want to use you for their own ends. That's why some famous people isolate themselves from others for their own protection. This, in turn, shrinks the circle of people in their lives—so there are fewer people really loving them.

The voices of American evangelicalism aren't far behind this cultural trend toward seeking worldly greatness to define success. This is why I call it our "Great" BIG problem: Churches have followed the culture's lead in defining greatness as bigness. Whatever the pursuit, great equals big. While the reasons Christian periodicals produce annual lists of the fastest growing and largest churches in America are not always clear to the average person, young pastors are immediately drawn to the implied definition of a "great" church. In my seminary experience, the missionary William Carey was often quoted, "Expect great things from God; attempt great things for God!" Unfortunately, for many going into ministry, greatness is not the content of their character, but the size of their impact or the spread of their influence. American greatness is not the same thing as Christian greatness.

Important people confer upon others credibility, which has historically been why prominent church leaders have had such little accountability—everyone is potentially feeding their own need for significance at the trough of celebrity affirmation. I have spoken with multiple pastors who said their desire to be close to the glow of a celebrity pastor's aura kept them from speaking truth to them, for fear of being cut off. Being close to someone famous and important transmits a feeling of affirmation and a growing fear of losing this emotional drug.

Ohio State University communications professor Brad Bushman has studied this subject at length and discovered that boosts to self-esteem and praise from powerful people have the properties of addiction. "We've done some research showing some people would rather have a boost in self-esteem than get money or eat their favorite food or see their favorite friends. They just can't stop seeking praise. It has this addictive quality."[10] I certainly can testify to the truth of this research.

Author Jen Kim wrote in *Psychology Today*, "The more I read about celebrity, the less I think it's what I actually want. Of course, there is a certain allure to having tons of money or access to ultra-exclusive people and events, but what I really want (and I imagine what most people want) is to feel significant and unique."[11] This honest answer is what so many Christians (including many Christian leaders) fail to acknowledge. It's embarrassing to tell others that your motives are twisted or in conflict. Christian leaders will be rejected by some as defective and unqualified for feeling this way. But a failure to honestly confess has brought disaster to church communities, and will continue to do so.

IT HAS ALWAYS BEEN EVER THUS

There is truth to the oft-repeated justification for the church's success syndrome. It has been like this since the days of the apostles. We see it in Saint Paul's condemnation of factions based on powerful leaders. Human nature jockeys for position in the Lord's future kingdom. In the Gospel of Mark, Jesus's earthly ministry is experiencing great success. Massive crowds are attending the events, the miraculous feeding of thousands occurs twice, people are being healed, and demons are being cast out. Yet, in all of this excitement, Jesus's disciples were thinking of their own glory.

James and John (the sons of Zebedee), who had recently seen Jesus's transfiguration, hatched a plan they thought would secure their prominence in God's kingdom. They asked Jesus if they could sit at His right and left when He eventually ascended to His throne. Jesus told them that they didn't know what they were asking, and they didn't. As far as they knew, Jesus was going to set up a kingdom on earth, and they were asking for prized positions in the administration. But Jesus warned them that such glory comes only after great suffering. Then He would ascend to the throne in heaven and receive all power and authority from the Father.

They clearly didn't get the picture. The other disciples were none too fond of James and John when they heard what they'd asked. As they bickered over who would get more power and authority, Jesus had to intervene with a quick seminar on "Greatness, the Jesus Way."

> Jesus called them together and said, "You know that those who are regarded as rulers of the Gentiles lord it over them, and their high officials exercise authority over them. Not so with you. Instead, whoever wants to become great among you must be your servant, and whoever wants to be first must be slave of all. For even the Son of Man did not come to be served, but to serve, and to give his life as a ransom for many."
> **Mark 10:42-45**

Here's where the GOSPEL intersects with REAL LIFE: Jesus is talking to those who have experienced Him. He's giving a new command to those who have been touched by His humility. He is calling those who claim to be His followers to imitate HIS greatness—a greatness that is found in service and sacrifice.

Jesus taught that there is more joy in giving than receiving. Pastor Rick Warren echoes these thoughts: "God determines

> "**God determines your greatness by how many people you serve, not how many people serve you.**" — Rick Warren

your greatness by how many people you serve, not how many people serve you."[12] From this passage, we derive the Christian reality that all gifts of leadership are meant to serve others, and that Christlike greatness is being a servant of all. Jesus contrasts the worldly definition of greatness with His own. Among those who are not God's people (referred to as Gentiles, before Jesus died for the sins of the whole world), if you're great, you're a ruler of people.

We see this in our era: The rich and powerful have servants. If you're a member of the economic lower or middle class, your first experience with being served like this can be uncomfortable. My brother-in-law's business associate once flew us to an event in a private plane. When we arrived at the private airport, a handful of working-class people like me ran onto the tarmac and rolled out a red carpet for us to walk on once we reached the bottom of the airstair. It was a little embarrassing. But people of privilege expect that they should rule, and others should serve. Jesus turns this notion on its head. If you want to be great in His kingdom, you won't be sitting at His right and left as James and John had tried to negotiate. Whoever wants the distinction of being great in Jesus's realm must be the servant of all.

The late Dr. Henri Nouwen (a Catholic priest and scholar who left his Ivy League job to live among the severely handicapped) noticed this appetite in himself. He said he found himself speaking to thousands of people about humility, and at the same time wondering what they were thinking of him. Ever since we ceased abiding in God's presence, because of our sinful nature (more to come on this in the next chapter), we have all desired glory. And our longing for glory led us astray. When Satan misled the first human beings, he convinced them that if they disobeyed God and ate from the Tree of the Knowledge of Good and Evil, they'd be like God.

From the beginning, we were made to enjoy God's glory. Instead, we have continually attempted to rob God of His claim to it. We often forget that we are created beings, crafted by God, gifted by God, and constantly protected by God. And when we forget who and whose we are, we foolishly try to make our life's work and relationships about our own glory. American culture describes our pursuit of higher levels of greatness as "upward mobility." Scripture says that Jesus has something else in mind for us, something Dr. Nouwen famously called "downward mobility."

In his book Out of Solitude, Nouwen wrote:

> "When we start being too impressed by the results of our work, we slowly come to the erroneous conviction that life is one large scoreboard where someone is listing the points to measure our worth. And before we are fully aware of it, we have sold our soul to the many grade-givers. That means we are not only in the world, but also of the world."[13]

BLIND TO OUR OWN SIN

A megachurch pastor stood in front of the other ministers he was supposedly leading and announced, "I'm not here to be your friend and don't have time to take your calls. I may not know much about being a pastor, but I know a lot about leadership." He was serious. Success had made this "minister of the gospel" blind to his own sin of pride. I was saddened to hear it come from his mouth, mostly because I remember how twisted my sense of value got when I experienced ministry success. Like a rich person, one can easily be fooled into thinking they have more to do with their success than they really do. I read about a minister who was fired from his megachurch because, according to him, "his character couldn't keep up with his gifting." Even in the announcement of his colossal failure, he found a way to boast. We're so unbelievably broken.

I raised money for a nonprofit at one point in my career. While doing so, I met with wealthy people and realized how difficult it must be for them to keep a balanced perspective about who they really are. Rich people are used to people giving them what they want, when they want it. They're used to people telling them what they want to hear, and never hearing something that would jeopardize their willingness to donate money. Thus, many wealthy individuals end up thinking that everything they say must be a stroke of genius, and that most of their success is due to their superior skills. Ministers who grow large ministries face the same risks. They might begin to believe their own press and think they are the real difference makers. "Sure, we need the Holy Spirit," they say, "but the Holy Spirit uses gifted people like me." For some reason, they fail to realize that the Holy Spirit uses them IN SPITE of their lack of giftedness or character.

The 1999 film *The Pirates of Silicon Valley* portrays the story of tech giants Bill Gates and Steve Jobs. In a critical scene, Gates and his partners meet with IBM to negotiate the leasing of Microsoft software for Big Blue's machines. Unbeknownst to IBM, this would become the primary billion-dollar revenue source for this virtually unknown startup. In the middle of the negotiation, filmmakers freeze the action. Then, the actor portraying Microsoft executive Steve Ballmer turns to the camera to announce to the audience that this was the moment that made the company. A colossal blunder by a corporate behemoth. In the end, a handful of men became the wealthiest people in the world because of a lucky break.

Almost everyone has been surprisingly (and undeservedly) given a break that made them successful. This is true for EVERYONE in ministry. Everyone depends on God's grace, which is what Jesus was saying when He explained that apart from Him, we can do nothing. Why is it so easy for us to forget that simple reality? It's partly because our sinful pride wants to believe that we are special compared to others. We want others to revere us. We want others to forget that God created us and gave us these talents.

Los Angeles is home to a host of old theaters. In Hollywood's golden age, these theaters had grand marquees that featured the names of stars in BIG, bold lights. Isn't this the dream of every performer, to see their name "up in lights"? This shouldn't be the Christian's dream, and certainly not that of a Christian minister. Our dream should be seeing Jesus's name exalted. Our job? To be the one hanging the letters on the sign. Those in ministry are especially susceptible to inviting everyone to the "Jesus movie," and then trying to steal His applause. We combat this by remembering the grace we preach. God has made us—He is the potter and we are the clay. God has providentially ordained our every step.

No individual comes to Jesus unless the Holy Spirit draws him or her. Every grace is given in spite of us, not because of us. It is unconditional. God made you, values you, and wants to use you. But He wants you to serve Him in a way that makes much of Jesus and little of yourself. He wants others to see Jesus's disposition in you. That happens when you sacrifice for others, as He did. He is great because He gave His life as a ransom for many. And Jesus is a BIG deal because He made Himself nothing and took on the role of a servant.

"In your relationships with one another, have the same mindset as Christ Jesus: Who, being in very nature God, did not consider equality with God something to be used to his own advantage; rather, he made himself nothing by taking the very nature of a servant, being made in human likeness. And being found in appearance as a man, he humbled himself by becoming obedient to death—even death on a cross! Therefore God exalted him to the highest place and gave him the name that is above every name, that at the name of Jesus every knee should bow, in heaven and on earth and under the earth, and every tongue acknowledge that Jesus Christ is Lord, to the glory of God the Father."
Philippians 2:5-11

SIX.

The Status Struggle

I was 25 when I saw my first Ku Klux Klan rally. I had moved to Ocala, Florida, in 1990 with my new bride. I was there to help get the city's first Christian FM radio station on the air, serving as its program director and morning show host. Ocala is a very conservative Central Florida city. Other than its historic equestrian business (some of history's great horses have been bred and trained there), the city doesn't have a major industry. People who like quiet, country living find their way to Ocala. Many of these residents are retirees. There are also many churches, and a high percentage of the population identifies as Christian.

Both my wife and I were raised in the Northeast and had heard tales of the KKK. We had seen movies where the Klan was portrayed, but we'd never seen a Klansman in person. All of a sudden, there they were in the town square, dozens of KKK guys in their creepy white costumes and dunce caps. Apart from the startling first-time sighting, what stunned us most was the absence of any protest group. There was not a soul shouting down these racist, anti-Semitic fearmongers. No churches were there to graciously confront the demonic twisting of Old Testament passages to support white supremacy or unbiblical notions of segregation. Where were they?

The silence was deafening.

A more important question: "Where was I?" In my self-righteous indignation, I failed to see myself as part of the problem. Our second tip for our Christian climb of faith is, "Know your limitations." That admonition isn't only about avoiding active disobedience to Scripture or creating helpful safety guardrails for life (such as, if you're an alcoholic, perhaps it's best that you don't work as a bartender). Knowing our limitations is specifically about humility. It's about knowing how broken we are, which should make us aware of our tendency to be passively disobedient. Loving others is an action, and when we don't actively love others, we are sinning every bit as much as when we DO something we regret.

Additionally, part of our mandate as Christians is to see ourselves accurately in relation to others. I hope to show that part of vital Christian spirituality is humbling ourselves before our world. Part of the solution to becoming a strong Christian or vibrant church is helping the less fortunate and the marginalized. When we have failed to do this, it's often because we are struggling with our status. I can speak only for myself, but I like being first, and I also like feeling I'm the most important person in the room. I don't think it's a stretch to generalize that we are all fond of being the MVP or the VIP. It is normative to see the word "elite" used to describe the most difficult places to get into or the highest level of accomplishment a person can obtain.

Those who have obtained a high level of status will comment privately that this thrill is short-lived. Once elite status is achieved, we must do one of two things:

1. Confront the emptiness of completing the climb, only find it didn't bring the happiness we hoped for.
2. Start climbing again.

Like other aspects of our broken human nature, our impulse to follow our instincts often leads us away from God's plan for us. Discontent is a poison that keeps us from enjoying what we have, and it further distorts our view of who we are before God and other people. As the Puritan Thomas Watson said of discontentment, "A drop or two of vinegar will sour a whole glass of wine."[1]

This compulsion to obtain a high status or see ourselves as higher than others runs counter to the Christian calling to do nothing out of selfish ambition. We're taught to humbly value others above ourselves, not look to our own interests, but to the interests of others.[2] If we're going to love others well, we are commanded to be completely humble, gentle, and patient, and to bear with one another in love.[3] Loving others by putting their interests ahead of ours takes intentionality. It's also trusting God to, somehow, meet our needs. (His plan is that others will willingly serve us.)

It's deceptively easy to fail to put others first, while maintaining that we've done nothing wrong. If we want to thrive as Christ followers, we must follow Christ's example and lower ourselves. I believe our distance from the needy is one of convenience. Our sense of entitled comfort has deprived us of an opportunity to experience Jesus, who said that whatever we do for the lowest of society, we do for Him. In James 2:1-13, the apostle James warned the first-century church to resist their selfish tendency to show favoritism to the rich. We encounter Christ through our humility before our world, specifically before those who are marginalized by society.

LIFE LESSONS FROM A LOWLY NUN

Until her death in 1997, a Roman Catholic nun known to the world as Mother Teresa spent the bulk of her life serving the poorest of the poor in Calcutta, India. In 1950, at age 40, she started her own order, the Missionaries of Charity, which spawned hundreds of missions around the world. For her efforts, she won multiple awards, including the Nobel Peace Prize. But she didn't serve the poor to win accolades or fame; instead, she said all of her sacrifice was just one way to experience Jesus's presence. She wrote:

> "Works of love are always a means of becoming closer to
> God. Look at what Jesus did in His life on earth! He spent
> it just doing good. I remind the sisters that three years
> of Jesus's life were spent healing the sick and the lepers,
> children and other people; and that's' exactly what we're
> doing, spreading the Gospel through our actions."[4]

One part of my Catholic upbringing I've clung to is a portion of the corporate prayer of confession recited each Sunday. The "Penitential Act" I memorized as a child said in part, "I confess to Almighty God, and to you my brothers and sisters, that I have sinned of my own fault. In my thoughts and in my words. In what I have done and what I have failed to do." I'm fairly cognizant of my active sins, things I have done. As a highly emotional person, I have a real sensitivity to when someone is withdrawing from me because of something I did. On the other hand, I'm often clueless about my passive sins. There are many times on any given day where I fail to love people, and I often don't know it until someone points it out.

However, our passivity regarding helping those in need or fighting for the mistreated is disobedience. Social justice movements have adopted the slogan that "Silence is violence." The spirit of the mantra is that passivity in the face of injustice makes a person an accessory to it. Some of my more painful relationship endings outside of church were with those I thought were friends, but when they had a chance to defend me, they remained silent. Their concern for their own regard, well-being, or comfort caused them to remain quiet when they knew something fishy was going on. While I've had to work to forgive these people, those relationships are forever changed because trust is no longer present. I could hope that the next time they'd go to bat for me, but the unreliability of their response keeps me cautiously distant from them.

Incidentally, this is how many of my African American friends characterize their relationship with theologically conservative white churches, people, and even some of their white friends. By God's grace they're doing their best to forgive them for their general passivity in the face of racial injustice, but the unreliability of their response has made them keep their distance. As Martin Luther King Jr. said, "In the end, we will remember not the words of our enemies, but the silence of our friends." The impoverished souls we have passively ignored and/or blamed for their circumstances will feel the same reluctance toward other Christians. It will take a long time for many to return a place where they trust that those who have hurt them through indifference are safe to be around.

SERVING THE KING AS AN AMBASSADOR

I have a favorite scene from HBO's *John Adams* miniseries. Once America's war for independence was won, Congress sent Adams to England to be the first U.S. ambassador to the Court of St. James. As Adams (portrayed by award-winning actor Paul Giamatti) approaches the king's throne, he trembles with fear because of his unfamiliarity with British customs. Once he speaks, however, his training in oratory and his eloquent vocabulary (which some peers found arrogant) serve him well, given the auspiciousness of the circumstances. A group of rebellious citizens were approaching the king to reestablish friendly relations. The erudite John Adams was made for just such an occasion.

Christians are God's ambassadors, representing the Lord's disposition toward all who are made in His image. Believers have already seen Jesus do this for us, serving as our ambassador before the throne of our Heavenly Father. Our Savior continues to intercede for us and serve as our mediator. By extension, we are now to represent our Lord to humanity. God wants those who suffer in this life to know that He is there among them, through the presence of His children. Our inaction, unfortunately, implies to those in pain that God is emotionally disconnected or absent.

The evidence that one truly walks with God is, in part, doing justice and loving mercy.[5] Scripture describes this as a "living faith." Saint James calls a faith without care for the poor not mostly dead, but "dead."

> What good is it, my brothers and sisters, if someone claims
> to have faith but has no deeds? Can such faith save them?
> Suppose a brother or a sister is without clothes and daily food.
> If one of you says to them, "Go in peace; keep warm and well
> fed," but does nothing about their physical needs, what good
> is it? In the same way, faith by itself, if it is not accompanied
> by action, is dead. But someone will say, "You have faith; I
> have deeds." Show me your faith without deeds, and I will
> show you my faith by my deeds. You believe that there is one
> God. Good! Even the demons believe that—and shudder.
> **James 2:14-19**

Can you think of a harsher warning than what James has issued here? It's as if he's saying, "So, you think your belief in a higher power is sufficient to please God? Well, professor, demons believe that. Their response to God's existence is to recognize His power and be scared. That's compared to you, who seem convinced that God is your buddy, and yet you attend to very little of what the Father commands you to do." To be clear, the New Testament doesn't claim that good works produce the right to be in relationship with God. Relationship with God is a gift given to those who receive the forgiveness offered through Christ's death. (We'll explore this concept further in the next chapter.)

That said, James (who is the Saint James after which the court of England is named), says authentic Christianity doesn't exist unless good works are present in our lives. Passivity isn't an option. For too long, many of us have had a "devil may care" attitude about mercy and justice. We have used our correct theology of "works are produced by grace" to justify a Christianity that lacks passion for the "least of these." Instead of deep sadness and a desire to change our apathy, we've managed to take cover behind Jesus's statement that "the poor you will always have with you."[6]

This laissez-faire attitude is a far cry from the passionate pursuit of meeting the needs of the poor, which we see throughout the New Testament. So big was the early church's ministry to the poor that the Lord instituted the office of deacons (servants) to lead others in this ministry. This was no minor church program.[7] In Larry Hurtado's research about the early church, he writes, "Early Christianity of the first three centuries was a different, even distinctive, kind of religious movement in the cafeteria of religious options of the time. That is not simply my historical judgment; it is

> "
> **For too long, many of us have had a 'devil may care' attitude about mercy and justice. We have used our correct theology of 'works are produced by grace' to justify a Christianity that lacks passion for the 'least of these.'"**

what people of the time thought as well. In the eyes of many in the Roman era, Christianity was odd, even objectionably so."[8] Hurtado points out that the distinguishing marks of the church were that it was multiethnic and that it included people of a lower social status.

AVOIDING THE LITTLE PEOPLE

A few years ago, the pastor of one of America's largest churches made national news after it was discovered that he had engaged in affairs with several women in his community, over a period of years. As the sordid details became public—and others were astounded by the sheer breadth of the deception—I noticed something. In one report, a local real estate developer spoke of his conversion to Christianity and how this megachurch pastor was so easily accessible to him. I found that odd, as other reports indicated that no one at the church ever saw him. If you wanted a meeting with this celebrity pastor, you'd have to wait months. This preferential treatment of the rich and famous is condemned in Scripture. But it's common among Christian leaders who are feeding their souls by being part of the "in crowd." Unfortunately, this kind of restricted pastoral access makes the influential person sink deeper into the illusion that "I'm different. I'm special."

I've talked with wealthy or gifted people, and I sometimes hear echoes of superiority in their tone. They might criticize those who are less educated or less sophisticated. They seem to have forgotten how they got to where they are. The church is composed of people that the Lord calls

> "**The church is composed of people that the Lord calls His body. When even a few of those members forget that all that they have is by grace, it negatively affects the entire body. Pride is a virus, and once it infects the system, it weakens it, sometimes rendering it ineffective.**"

His body. When even a few of those members forget that all that they have is by grace, it negatively affects the entire body. Pride is a virus, and once it infects the system, it weakens it, sometimes rendering it ineffective. I believe that our passivity toward those in need or those disenfranchised by systems and cultures is largely due to our forgetting how we arrived at our position. We forget that our position of influence is God-given, not earned. And we are supposed to use that position to serve others—and not the other way around.

People born to families of wealth and influence, those born in countries that are safely governed by a coherent set of constitutional laws, or those who have benefited from a particular genetic code are foolish to forget that all we have was given by God, to steward on His behalf. Grace isn't just the gospel concept that provides forgiveness to the undeserving. Properly understood and applied, grace is at the root of every step of life. Humility before our world means that the culture will see the church not as powerful, but as servants. Jesus calls us to "great" humility. We are here to serve the less fortunate, and not the other way around.

Economic injustice happens when the wealthy forget God gave them stewardship of resources so they can serve the less fortunate. They forget that by grace they have been given opportunities that their workers haven't. Perhaps they were blessed by God with greater intelligence by virtue of their genetics. This intelligence was a creative action that God oversaw. The heart of the matter for Christians is to remember who is creating and who is benefiting. God created us and blessed the affluent, so we are benefiting. Thus, we serve God out of gratitude. Workers are creating, and the owners are benefiting. Hence, they are called to serve the workers out of gratitude. If you take credit and assume glory for the work of another, this is dishonest. In publishing, it's called plagiarism. In the business world, it's referred to as intellectual property theft. For heads of people who work to accomplish the leader's goals, it's forgetting who is creating and who is benefiting.

Hence, it seems unthinkable that someone who was born

into and inherited massive amounts of wealth would ever forget the long list of gifts and benefits they'd graciously received from God. But it happens all the time. If we forget or neglect the fact that God created us, we see ourselves as the masters of our fate and the captains of our souls. Our foolish pride makes us forget how we got where we are. Trace the success story of the average Westerner; did he or she have any advantages that people born in developing nations don't enjoy? A growing number of young people are more sensitive than ever to economic and cultural wrongdoing. When they see a church that is too busy to help those in need, they see people who think they're better than others.

> " **A growing number of young people are more sensitive than ever to economic and cultural wrongdoing. When they see a church that is too busy to help those in need, they see people who think they're better than others."**

THE SHEEP AND THE GOATS

The proliferation of television and internet news outlets and the light-speed transmission of information is catapulting global movements as never before. This is a tremendous opportunity for the church, which has been commanded to make mercy and justice a high priority. However, when the church and its people forget that they are recipients of overwhelming amounts of grace, they often forget the needs of the less fortunate. At worst, they will look down their nose and blame these poor souls for their plight without recognizing that some have disabilities and addictions that others don't have to face. In my lifetime, church organizations have been good at setting up social service agencies. But individual Christians have not been as generous with their attitudes toward the less fortunate. Sadly, I confess that I have sometimes been one of them. It is fairly easy for those who believe they're Christians to passively ignore the issues of mercy and justice and think they're all good with the Father. Scripture warns us otherwise.

Jesus spoke in parables for a couple of reasons, which He explains in Matthew 10. And we can assume that humble people learn better when they have word pictures. In His parable of the sheep and the goats, Jesus addresses mercy, justice, and judgment. There is an important connection between what we've been talking about in this chapter and this parable.

"When the Son of Man comes in his glory, and all
the angels with him, then he will sit on his glorious
throne. Before him will be gathered all the nations, and
he will separate people one from another as a shepherd
separates the sheep from the goats. And he will place the
sheep on his right, but the goats on the left.
Then the King will say to those on his right, 'Come,
you who are blessed by my Father, inherit the kingdom
prepared for you from the foundation of the world. For
I was hungry and you gave me food, I was thirsty and
you gave me drink, I was a stranger and you welcomed
me, I was naked and you clothed me, I was sick and you
visited me, I was in prison and you came to me.' Then
the righteous will answer him, saying, 'Lord, when did
we see you hungry and feed you, or thirsty and give you
drink? And when did we see you a stranger and welcome
you, or naked and clothe you? And when did we see you
sick or in prison and visit you?'
And the King will answer them, 'Truly, I say to you, as
you did it to one of the least of these my brothers,
you did it to me.'
"Then he will say to those on his left, 'Depart from me, you
cursed, into the eternal fire prepared for the devil and his
angels. For I was hungry and you gave me no food, I was

> thirsty and you gave me no drink, I was a stranger and
> you did not welcome me, naked and you did not clothe me,
> sick and in prison and you did not visit me.
> "Then they also will answer, saying, 'Lord, when did we
> see you hungry or thirsty or a stranger or naked or sick
> or in prison, and did not minister to you?' Then he will
> answer them, saying, 'Truly, I say to you, as you did
> not do it to one of the least of these, you did not do it to
> me.' And these will go away into eternal punishment, but
> the righteous into eternal life."
> **Matthew 25:31-46**

We know that justice matters to Jesus because He speaks of it often. He addresses justice in this parable, which details the final judgment of all humans. Some people will spend eternity in God's presence, and others will spend eternity apart from God in what Scripture calls hell. I don't argue with people who want to debate about whether hell will literally be fire and sulfur, because the point of the passage is that some people will not be with God. Eternal regret for missing out on living with my Creator would feel like hell. Living in a place where God didn't exist and injustice was free to reign, with the worst parts of human nature running amok (picture the most violent prison in history)? That sounds like hell to me.

Jesus's parable gives insight into the way He'll determine who is an authentic follower of His and who is not. First, the "sheep" will be saved, but they are humble about it. They don't claim they deserve salvation. The people on His right receive their eternal blessing based solely on God's grace. However, there is evidence that they've lived their lives in a genuine state of God's grace: They helped the least of those in society. Conversely, the "goats" think they're friends with God, but they aren't. He says, "I never knew you." These people thought that by simply believing that God exists, or by going through some religious motions, they were on good terms with God. These people are incredulous that they're being left out, completely clueless that the lack of God's grace in their lives was evidenced by their cluelessness about the plight of the least of those in society.

The notion of a final judgment is contained in Scripture, and it's been part of our ecumenical creeds. The Nicene Creed says "to judge the living and the dead." Some theological progressives sometimes feign agreement with the Council of Nicaea, which produced the creed in 325 A.D. However, with further discussion, one discovers that they don't believe in a final "judgment" at all. Or at least one like that described in Matthew 25. There is an enormous problem in the theology of those who deny an eternal judgment. In their estimation, because God is love, He won't judge anyone and sentence them to an eternity apart from His presence. Without justice, the world's most notorious criminals and despots would spend eternity in the presence of Jesus. If this anti-Nicene Creed understanding is to be believed, there won't be a "*Depart from me, you cursed*" moment in the afterlife. Not even in the worst cases of evil in human history. The Son of Man will issue a proverbial, "Fuhgeddaboudit! I hope you feel bad. Now, enter into your rest." God is passive. There is no justice.

We've made the case that God is as displeased with passive sin as He is with active sin. Judgment will come for those who don't demonstrate their genuine faith by caring for the least of these. Why? Because God's mercy and justice are displayed when those who have been given much enable those who haven't to experience God's love, provision, mercy, and JUSTICE. If there is no penalty paid for sin, injustice at the cosmic level will take place. We've seen in Scripture (and chapter four) that we're all sinful and without hope apart from an atoning sacrifice. Some of the theological progressives I've encountered contend that this notion of judgment is not real.

Here's my question: If there is no judgment for our sins (passive or active), what risk is there in my rejection of their re-created definitions of Christianity? If there is no justice for the people they think are being mistreated by orthodox Christian theology, what's to keep me from remaining entrenched in my position? If God won't eventually make all things right and bring justice to the oppressed, what hope do we have that He will engage with humanity to correct justice today? You may retort, "He wants to exact justice through us." I agree. But if He's willing to bring about justice and hold the oppressor accountable through us, why is it unthinkable that He HIMSELF would do the same? Jesus says in this parable that He will. God is not passive-aggressive. The Almighty is upset by injustice, and He's not too timid to do the difficult work of holding human beings accountable.

I HATE PEOPLE WHO DON'T LOVE OTHERS

I saw a bumper sticker proclaiming MEAN PEOPLE SUCK. Bumper-to-bumper traffic gives an L.A. resident plenty of time to read bumper stickers. I've observed that there are three types of car owners when it comes to bumper stickers. First, there is the NO STICKERS ANY TIME car owner. This person will never put any sticker on their car, for any reason. Second, there is the MY KID IS AN HONOR STUDENT car owner. Whether it's the honor roll, the marching band, or the athletic team, these folks put only one bumper sticker on their car so they can honor a child.

The third kind is what I call the I'M ANXIOUS AND POLITICALLY ACTIVE car owner. This person covers the rear of their car with bumper stickers expressing outrage about their political issues and enemies. I confess that often I find myself pulling up next to them to see what they look like. I also get a little nervous about how others view the church when there is a Christian bumper sticker in amongst the protest messages. If you are one of those whose anxieties are stirred by the politics of our day, you have my great sympathy. I can't watch more than five minutes of cable news at a time without feeling my blood pressure rise. But as your friend let me say, covering the rear of your car with bumper stickers significantly depreciates the value of your car.

As I've already made clear, I believe that a Christian's ultra-close association with any political movement is detrimental to the church and its public witness. However, many who have abandoned the evangelical church mischaracterize the essence of the gospel and use that misrepresentation as an excuse to ignore large sections of the Scriptures. In one response to an article condemning evangelical Christian support of Donald Trump in 2016, a therapist who proudly characterized herself as an "exvangelical" (someone who used to cling to theologically orthodox beliefs) asserted that a fearmongering president is congruous with a version of Christianity that believes in a final judgment. Her perspective on a theologically conservative understanding of the Scripture was that it produced a fearful, bigoted, and punitive culture. She wrote:

> "A theology that continues to send millions to be tortured in hell necessitates a fundamental traumatic split in the psyche. It represents the very heart of cognitive dissonance, and results in a lack of empathy based in fear and judgment. In this equation—perfect love does not cast out fear, because this version of God is based in threat."

I'm sorry that this sister has not comprehended the gospel of grace that many teach, which is contained in the New Testament. I'm not certain why she thinks Jesus died on a cross. Was Jesus killed arbitrarily, without any reason? I imagine that the abuse she has heard about from her therapist's chair has reinforced her misconception about sin and judgment as it is taught in the Scriptures. For clarity's sake, a final judgment for sins is about justice.

Here's one huge problem for the "exvangelical": They want it both ways. They want to use God's Word to combat misogyny (I do too), racism (I do too), violence toward LGBTQ people (I do too), and many other forms of injustice. But when it comes to their own moral transgressions, or other violations of God's law, they act like the Bible is suddenly unknowable. They usually contend that neither the Old nor the New Testament is completely reliable (more coming about this later in this book) except when they want to posit, as our therapist friend did, that "love casts out all fear." But that was said by the apostle John, nine verses after he also said:

> "This is how God showed his love among us: He sent his
> one and only Son into the world that we might live through
> him. This is love: not that we loved God, but that he loved
> us and sent his Son as an atoning sacrifice for our sins."
> **1 John 4:18**

God does require active love from His people and we are not to judge those outside the church.[9] However, in our brokenness we can correctly point out injustice, but then quickly descend into impatience with our Christian brothers and sisters, an impatience we claim to abhor. We want others to be patient with us in our struggles, but we are quick to condemn people and churches who are on a journey where they become more like Jesus—a narrow trail that doesn't end until we see our Savior face to face. The apostle Paul wrote:

> "When I was a child, I talked like a child, I thought like a
> child, I reasoned like a child. When I became a man, I put
> the ways of childhood behind me. For now we see only a
> reflection as in a mirror; then we shall see face to face. Now
> I know in part; then I shall know fully, even as I am fully
> known. And now these three remain: faith, hope and
> love. But the greatest of these is love."
> **1 Corinthians 13:11-13**

The practice of humility is not easy. To be humble, we must continually see ourselves in light of the gospel. Because of our broken, sinful state, we don't deserve to live in God's presence, and we lack the moral ability to earn that right. Yet, God adores His children and has offered to forgive them for their nature and their actions, but the requirement is humility. However, if we want to receive forgiveness and be reconciled to God, we must admit our need for forgiveness by confessing our sins. 1 John 1:9 -10 states:

*"If we confess our sins, he is faithful and just and will
forgive us our sins and purify us from all unrighteousness.
If we claim we have not sinned, we make him out to be a
liar and his word is not in us."*

Subsequent to humbly receiving mercy, and in order to see reality clearly instead of through our blurred, distorted view, we need God's grace and strength to trust His Word about which way is up, down, right, or left. We'll also need the continual reassurance of His love for us so that when we stubbornly refuse to follow His commands, we'll realize that, as His redeemed children, we can run to Him instead of away. In the absence of comprehending our weakness, we will foolishly believe that we can handle life's challenges without God. But only in Him are the weak made strong. For us to get stronger spiritually, we must know our limitations through growing humility.

TIP #2 – Know your limitations
Spiritual strength develops with growing humility.

Tip #3: Don't lose sight of the path

Spiritual confidence deepens with
gospel clarity.

My senior year of high school was amazing. My basketball teammates and I won our league championship, as did our baseball team. As I mentioned before, at the beginning of that year, I finally decided to follow Jesus after a lifetime of church attendance and many attempts of trying to be good on my own strength. A couple of my teammates were vocal Christians, and one guy had a particularly stellar reputation as a believer. His name was Mark. Unlike him, it took me a while to let go of my hard-partying habits. Mark was recognized by everyone for being a straight arrow who avoided alcohol, and I don't remember seeing him at the parties where drinking took place. My friendship with Mark provided me some much-needed accountability.

Like many in my generation, my final year of high school also included a senior trip. This annual ritual was a reward for those who made it to graduation. The trip was notorious for being a week of relatively hard partying, even though the senior class sponsors tried to curb the practice. It wasn't uncommon for students to hide alcohol or marijuana in their bags. Some would hide liquor in contact lens solution bottles to avoid getting caught. You might be wondering, "With all of those suitcases, how would sponsors discover something so well hidden?" This is where the plot thickens. At the pre-trip meeting with our class sponsors (teachers from the school), they informed us that on the first day of our trip, before the luggage was loaded onto the bus, one suitcase would be selected and searched. If any alcohol or drugs were found, the trip would be canceled for everyone.

The day of reckoning came, and the sea of suitcases on the parking lot grew until the last student checked in. Our entire senior class stood outside, nervously watching as Mr. Schnapp waded into the luggage to pick out his test suitcase. As he grabbed one of the bags, he hoisted it for all to see and asked, "Whose suitcase is this?" Mark raised his hand and said, "It's mine."

My writing skills cannot do justice to either the volume or the sheer joy contained in the cheer that followed! Every person in our class (many of whom were guilty of smuggling) knew they would enjoy this trip because of our class savior, my friend Mark. I can't even remember if they searched Mark's suitcase. That's how sterling his reputation was. This story illustrates the nature of the gospel of Jesus Christ. Unworthy people receive the opportunity to journey with their Creator, because One who is completely worthy makes it possible.

Tip #3 is "Don't lose sight of the path." In this section, we're going to talk about different aspects of gospel clarity, which is the third part of the Three Tips paradigm, along with "Never go alone" (genuine community) and "Know your limitations" (growing humility). What is "gospel clarity"? The Greek word for "gospel" is translated "good news." The gospel of the New Testament is God's restoration of His world, beginning with relationship reconciliation with the focal point of His creation, human beings. Spiritual confidence deepens with gospel clarity.

The good news of God's Kingdom is that He restores us to a right relationship with Himself through the gift of Jesus's life, death, and resurrection. By being transformed by the Holy Spirit's power, we who are in friendship with God once again become the means of shining His light into our world. As Jesus taught us to pray, "Thy kingdom come, thy will be done, on earth as it is in heaven." The result of genuine Christian conversion is a changed life, and, by extension, a changed world. These changes to individuals and cultures may slowly improve and then at times decline. They will never reach perfection until Jesus returns in glory. But we have been changed, because our new disposition inspires us to please God.

To say that the gospel is only about believers getting to heaven is incorrect. The gospel is us beginning our eternal life of fellowship with God right now. Because we've been reconciled with our heavenly Father, our disposition has been changed and we want to love Him. We show our love for God by loving Him as He's directed in Scripture and serving His purposes in the world. We love our neighbors. We serve the less fortunate and fight for justice. We worship God with a community of fellow believers. We share the gospel with others and introduce them to our gracious Jesus. We grow in our understanding of God's majesty through the study of His Word. These are the works of Jesus's kingdom.

All of that said, none of the transformation of genuine Christian conversion can take place unless we first clearly understand our need for forgiveness and restoration to God. Asking someone to change their behavior and be like Jesus if they haven't been converted by the Holy Spirit would be like asking a caterpillar to fly like a butterfly. Yes, the gospel is about more than converting people so they can say, "I'm saved." It is about transforming people and our world so that God's attributes and glory can be seen clearly.

However, we need "gospel clarity" to live the Christian life in a way that brings joy to us and love to God. "Don't lose sight of the path" means that we never forfeit the joy given to us by Jesus. We are His children by His grace alone, apart from any work we do. To that end, this section of the book will be divided into three chapters:

> **Chapter 7—The Message of Grace:** How do I know that I'm genuinely a Christian?
> **Chapter 8—The Motive of Love:** What compels Christians to live counter-culturally?
> **Chapter 9—The Mission of Christ:** What is God's mission for the church?

Many people have been raised in church, just as I was. However, like me when I was young, when someone asks them, "What does it mean to be a Christian?" they lack a clear, coherent, or comprehensive answer. I think I can help us formulate a good one.

SEVEN.

The Message of Grace

When my friend challenged me to hike up Mount Wilson to celebrate his 50th birthday (something I've yet to forgive him for), with each passing hour I kept getting the sense that we were lost. For all of its beauty and world's best weather, California's park system lacks sufficient funding for signage. Serious mountaineers would tell me the real problem is that I lack sufficient skills to navigate the wilderness. I concur. I have a friend whose fiancée got lost on a hike, and it turned into a national news story. In the end, she was rescued after many days, but anyone who has ventured into the wild without clarity about where they are going risks getting lost.

Getting off the path while curiously exploring—and then finding ourselves lost is a real possibility. This is why we're encouraged to keep sight of the path (assuming we are on the right one). "Don't lose sight of the path" means that we understand the fundamental realities of our faith in Jesus. "Gospel clarity" is knowing exactly what we believe and what it means to be a Christian. It is natural and healthy to be spiritually curious, and to continue growing in our knowledge and comprehension of truth. Danger arises when we wander so far from the path that Christ has marked that we forget what it was and how we find it.

What is Christianity? How do we define it so others will know what we mean? It has become profoundly difficult to do this. When famous ex-Christians become buddies with celebrities, it becomes even more so, as they are provided a huge stage to share their stories of shrugging off what they term a flawed religious system. In an era where people use polite phraseology such as "my truth" and "your truth," it is entirely possible for someone to say "I'm a Christian," but abide by a definition of Christianity that is 180 degrees from the one described in Scripture and by history.

We live in a religious and politically pluralistic culture, but theological truth is still discernible. We can certainly answer questions about the Christian faith from the Old and New Testaments. People may not want to believe this "version" of Christianity, but it is the Christianity from Scripture. The New Testament is the testimony of Jesus's apostles, validated by the early church leadership and authenticated as God's Word by virtue of the resurrection of Jesus Christ (more on this later).

From my life in multiple Christian denominations and my theological education, I believe I can distill a definition of "Christian" at its most basic. On issues of practice that have separated Christians (the hows of Christian living, worship, etc.), there is plenty of direction from Scripture telling us to be gracious to one another. But on the essentials of the gospel, there is a substantial reason why there must be a full-throated defense of what constitutes real Christianity. Our peace with God and our confidence about His revealed attributes are jeopardized when a biblical faith is altered.

Over 2,000 years, Christianity has arrived at consensus about certain doctrinal realities that make up our faith's non-negotiable truths. The creeds of the first millennium of church history have formed the backbone of Christian belief, and all of those creeds were founded on Scripture. The non-negotiables contained in these creeds weren't arbitrarily laid down but discovered to be interconnected and dependent on one another. Creeds and confessions are designed to give clarity about who God is, as described in Scripture.

When I was a kid, we played a game called "house of cards." We would build row upon row of playing cards until they became a small tower. Then, we'd take turns removing cards until someone removed one that was so important to the structure that its absence caused the tower to plummet. In the 1980s Hasbro began to market a game called Jenga to the world. This game was similar to the house of cards, but creating a tower was easier. Wooden blocks are cross-stacked in rows of three to erect a tower. The game consists of removing blocks, one by one, without making the entire structure collapse. The loser is the one who causes the structure to fall.

Some religious people recognize Scripture passages that conflict with cultural norms. And some academics read the Scriptures through their lens of "truth" and develop their own consensus about how to define Christianity. As a result, some who identify as Christian determine to remove a "piece" of Christianity that is challenging to defend. Sometimes this change of beliefs is to avoid a particular biblical mandate about resisting their own passions. On and on, the pieces get removed until the tower that was once their belief system collapses into a heap.

An entire industry now exists for celebrating those who have ceased embracing historical or biblical Christianity. It is true that within Christian orthodoxy there are many different denominations with varied interpretations of issues that theologians and historic creeds would deem "nonessential" to the good news. Sincere Christians disagree about all manner of Christian beliefs and should be gracious to one another in their differences. The Bible may be infallible, but we are not. We should approach nonessential doctrinal disputes with brothers and sisters in Christ with this attitude of humility.

However, these new rock stars make a good living proclaiming a different "gospel" that reduces Christianity to another system of religious good works, rather than reconciliation with God made possible through Christ's death. Often what drives some of these voices is not first and foremost an independent study of Scripture that brings about a change of their beliefs, but instead a desire to not appear foolish to others, which then brings about a change in how they interpret the Bible's morality claims. Not surprisingly, for many the Bible

> "If we aren't clear about how Scripture defines the gospel, it is difficult to spot the 'alternative' versions when they show up."

is characterized as having been their problem all along, and their rejection of its authority as the solution. If we aren't clear about how Scripture defines the gospel, it is difficult to spot the "alternative" versions when they show up.

GEM CLARITY VERSES THE FUGAZI

I was the most fortunate of people when I got engaged. My fiancée's cousin Laura lived in our city and happened to be a jeweler. That's a big break, and I've not forgotten her kindnesses to me, a poor disc jockey with almost no money. Diamonds get more expensive depending on their size and, more importantly, their clarity. My budget was on the "small size and bad clarity" end of the spectrum, but after Laura deducted her store's profit, I was able to get a high-quality ring that was previously out of my reach.

Trained diamond merchants can spot cheap stones right away with their naked eyes. But to truly judge gem quality, their tool of choice is a loupe, a small magnifying glass allowing them to see deep into the gem. To the untrained eye, it's impossible to determine a tiny diamond's value. Most couldn't tell the difference between a cubic zirconia and a real diamond. In much the same way, many who identify as churchgoers know little about what Christians believe. Therefore, they have difficulty recognizing when something isn't real.

This chapter's aim is to provide gospel clarity in three different ways. First, we're going to look at the message of the gospel as contained in the New Testament and describe how the apostles of Christianity defined saving faith. Second, we'll look at what makes authentic faith possible, the saving sacrifice of Jesus, the Lamb of God. Finally, we'll delve into the theological reality of who is a Christian by discussing the role of the Holy Spirit. This chapter should help you get a firm grasp on the nature of basic Christianity so you can distinguish the real thing from a forgery.

Tip #3 is, "Don't lose sight of the path." In popular nomenclature, "the path" is often referred to as a morality path, or a set of rules for our behavior. "Stay on the narrow path" is a way to say "behave carefully." However, in New Testament terms, the narrow path enables us to enjoy the benefits of being God's children. In the three tips paradigm, the trail is a metaphor for an eternal relationship with God, made possible by the gift of His Son. Losing sight of the trail is the equivalent of ceasing to use scriptural definitions of what enables someone to be reconciled to God. These doctrines have been summarized in the creeds of the first millennium.

THE CREED

I mentioned before that the Nicene Creed played a substantial role in my childhood church life. Each week we recited it as part of the worship service, so the creed was ground into my memory. Interestingly, some people distance themselves from Scripture's definitions of Christianity, yet claim an allegiance to creeds like the one created at the Council of Nicaea in 325 A.D. Presumably, these people avoid the prickly details of the New Testament (on subjects like sexual ethics and eternal judgment), and still hold an attachment to Christianity by professing adherence to the Nicene Creed.

If we look at the history of this creed's creation, we see that the New Testament letters of the apostles were central to the council's discussions and, presumably, seen as authoritative. If we break down the creed's doctrinal pieces, we see that it contains beliefs that can be offensive to some. In this chapter, we're going to use this creed to identify some of the most important pieces of the proverbial Jenga tower that represents the necessary components of genuine Christian faith.

The Nicene Creed was written in response to theological challenges that the late third-century church was facing. Factions had begun to gather around cult-type leaders who were breaking away from the understood teaching of the apostles (as contained in the apostolic historical accounts and letters).[1] We'll address more of this later, but by the time the Nicene Creed was written, the church had (for two centuries) collected writings from the Christian apostles, writings they considered authoritative. Granted, the discussion about the "canon" or official list of New Testament books was not concluded for a couple more centuries, but this was not a new list.

Theologian F.F. Bruce wrote:

> "The New Testament books did not become authoritative
> for the church because they were formally included in a
> canonical list. On the contrary, the church included them
> in her canon because she already regarded them as divinely
> inspired, recognizing their innate worth and apostolic
> authority, direct or indirect."[2]

In other words, if you're trying to avoid association with the New Testament, and attempting to hide behind the Nicene, Apostles', or some other creed, that might not be the best strategy.

The Council of Nicaea was significant in its time for two reasons. First, it was the first recorded churchwide council since the first-century council (cited in Acts) that determined that Gentiles were to be part of the church.[3] Second, Roman persecution of Christians had ended a dozen years earlier and brought a measure of peace to the empire. However, Arius, a rogue priest in Alexandria, Egypt, was leading many away from the long-understood doctrinal cornerstone that Jesus was the eternal God who became flesh.

Arius and his followers were teaching that Jesus had a beginning, created like every other part of God's world. Therefore, He was not eternally divine. While Christians had been freed from persecution by the Emperor Constantine, the division among them threatened the new peace of Rome. The emperor gathered more than 300 bishops from around the Roman Empire, with the goal of establishing doctrinal consensus about the nature of Jesus and a clear definition of the Trinity. This is the Nicene Creed as it appears in the 2019 Anglican Book of Common Prayer:

> We believe in one God, the Father, the Almighty,
> maker of heaven and earth, of all that is, visible
> and invisible.
> We believe in one Lord, Jesus Christ, the only begotten Son

of God, eternally begotten of the Father, God from God,
Light from Light, true God from true God, begotten, not
made, of one Being with the Father; through him all things
were made. For us and for our salvation he came down
from heaven, was incarnate from the Holy Spirit and the
Virgin Mary and was made man.
For our sake he was crucified under Pontius Pilate; he
suffered death and was buried. On the third day he rose
again in accordance with the Scriptures; he ascended into
heaven and is seated at the right hand of the Father. He
will come again in glory to judge the living and the dead,
and his kingdom will have
no end.
We believe in the Holy Spirit, the Lord, the giver of life,
who proceeds from the Father [and the Son], who with
the Father and the Son is worshiped and glorified, who
has spoken through the prophets. We believe in one
holy catholic and apostolic Church. We acknowledge
one Baptism for the forgiveness of sins. We look for the
resurrection of the dead, and the life of the world to come.
Amen.[4]

You may wonder why it matters if Jesus is truly God. Why is
it important that He was born by virtue of the Holy Spirit conceiving
Him in a woman who had never had sexual intercourse before? Did
He have to physically come back to life, or can we just say He is "alive
in spirit?" And why does the Holy Spirit need to proceed from the
Father and the Son? What does that mean? These are the proverbial
Jenga pieces I mentioned previously. Many people who identify as
Christians no longer recognize the importance of holding on to core
doctrines, assuming they know why they are called so in the first
place. As a result, they discard them and find that the entire structure
crashes.

As the annual Ligonier Ministries research study on theology pointed out in 2020, "It may be unsurprising that the majority of the general U.S. population rejects the deity of Christ, but now almost a third of evangelicals agree that He was merely a great teacher."[5] Why does this matter? Because this foundational misunderstanding of who Jesus is doesn't bode well for a person's future endurance in the faith. If Jesus isn't by nature God, having existed eternally before creation and now ruling from on high, why would anyone risk their lives or reputation professing to believe in Him? More important, when our clarity about God's nature is jeopardized because we don't realize Jesus perfectly reflects God's character, that reduces our joy. Without clarity about who Jesus is, we don't make the intellectual connection that Jesus, who was friends with sinners like me, is actually God. Our confidence in God's mercy and love is at stake. Again, spiritual confidence deepens with gospel clarity.

THE GOOD NEWS

As a child, the word "gospel" confused me. The readers at church would introduce passages by saying, "This is a reading from the Gospel According to [so-and-so]." I didn't know what a gospel was, so when people talked about "the gospel," I assumed they were talking about the Bible. As noted earlier, "gospel" simply means good news. The good news is that God came to rescue us by His grace, and not by our efforts. Any other "gospel," when closely examined, is not good news at all. The apostle Paul attempts to summarize the good news in his letter to the Roman Christians. I've cited this passage before, but here we'll refer to how the Council of Nicaea made their declarations to clarify some non-negotiables of faith. As we've seen, if you start pulling out pieces of Christian doctrine without regard to how their absence affects other beliefs, you could end up with nothing.

> *"There is no difference between Jew and Gentile, for all have sinned and fall short of the glory of God, and all are justified freely by his grace through the redemption that came by Christ Jesus. God presented Christ as a sacrifice of*

atonement, through the shedding of his blood—to be received
by faith. (emphasis mine) He did this to demonstrate his
righteousness, because in his forbearance he had left the sins
committed beforehand unpunished—he did it to demonstrate
his righteousness at the present time, so as to be just and the
one who justifies those who have faith in Jesus."
Romans 3:22b-26

Remember the fall? In Chapter Five we outlined the Christian doctrine of humanity's fall into sin, which separated humans from God. The first thing we see in this section of Romans 3 is the declaration of our shared spiritual predicament: We have "all have sinned and fall short of the glory of God." Human beings need saving. The Nicene Creed affirms this: "For us and for our salvation he came down from heaven." Perhaps you wonder what we need saving from? Paul says that Jesus came to save us from punishment for our wrongdoings. Just judges require that justice be done, even if their own children were the ones committing the offenses. A just God can be no different. Up to the time of Jesus, God had "left the sins committed beforehand unpunished."

Furthermore, if we do not, by faith in Jesus, receive His free pardon, we will continue in a state of separation from God for eternity. We will continue in a state of judgment. John's Gospel declares:

"Whoever believes in him is not condemned, but whoever
does not believe stands condemned already because they
have not believed in the name of God's one and only Son."
John 3:18

The Nicene Creed echoes this future judgment by King Jesus: "He ascended into heaven and is seated at the right hand of the Father. He will come again in glory to judge the living and the dead, and his kingdom will have no end."

So far, bad news. Lots of discussion about judgment and

> **"If we can see the true seriousness of our sin, we will no longer object to God's supposed severity but marvel at His mercy."**
> **— Dr. Vern Poythress**

sin. However, good news produces joy in light of the bad news. The celebration at the end of wars is joyous because of the horror of massive human death that preceded them. In this case, the reason the good news is so wonderful is that our souls were in jeopardy before God sent His Son to save us. As theologian Vern Poythress has written, "If we can see the true seriousness of our sin, we will no longer object to God's supposed severity but marvel at His mercy."[6]

While Romans 3:23 says we're all sinful and in danger of judgment, verse 24 adds that we "are justified freely by his grace through the redemption that came by Christ Jesus." Grace is defined as an unearned benefit. God offers the gift of salvation through a payment (redemption) that Jesus made on behalf of all who look to Him. The Nicene Creed says, "For our sake he was crucified under Pontius Pilate; he suffered death and was buried." Jesus's death wasn't primarily about showing what love looks like, although He did declare that giving your life for another is the greatest demonstration of love.[7]

John the Baptist called Jesus the "Lamb of God, who takes away the sin of the world!"[8] It is significant that John the apostle (whose historical account gives us the words of John the Baptist) also wrote the book of Revelation, which is peppered with references to Jesus as "the Lamb" who sits on the throne.[9] Why "the Lamb"? When the nation of Israel was freed from slavery to Egypt, the final plague the Lord sent to Pharaoh and that nation was death. The Jews were spared the Angel of Death's taking of their firstborn sons by sacrificing an innocent, spotless lamb. They were told to wipe the lamb's blood over their doorposts. God promised that when their homes were covered by the blood of this sacrifice, death would "pass over" them. When Israel celebrated this annual festival of remembrance, they were ordered to sacrifice a lamb and recall how God provided innocent lambs to spare them from death.

When Jesus is called "the Lamb of God," it's to announce that He is fulfilling an ancient Jewish hope for a Messiah to save them. God would save His people again by allowing an innocent to take our place. This time, Jesus would be the substitute, and when by faith we claim His blood to cover our lives, death "passes over" us. We're no longer in danger of death, or eternal separation from God. When Jesus "ascended into heaven," He presented His own blood as the atoning sacrifice for the sins of all who would ever humbly call out to Him for mercy. Scripture teaches that Jesus was perfect so that He could be the innocent, holy substitute for guilty, sinful humans. Theologian Charles Hodge wrote:

> "Christ, having offered Himself on the cross as a sacrifice
> for our sins, has passed through the heavens, there to
> appear before God in our behalf. He is, therefore, said to be
> the minister of the true tabernacle, which the Lord pitched
> and not man. His priestly office is now exercised in heaven,
> where He ever lives to intercede for us." [10]

This is where Scripture and the Nicene Creed help us to see the interconnectivity of non-negotiable beliefs. Aside from prophecies declaring that a virgin would conceive the Messiah (Isaiah 7:14 and Matthew 1:23), through His conception by the Holy Spirit, Jesus was protected from the stain of a sinful nature. Further, if Mary had previously had sex, there would for many remain a doubt about whether or not Joseph or another were the biological father. And if Jesus had an earthly biological father, he would be a mere human being with a sinful human nature that was passed onto him (see chapter four). A human being with a sinful nature would need to pay for his own sins and couldn't be a suitable substitute for others.

Most importantly, if Jesus wasn't the perfect sacrifice for our sins, those who believe in the God of the Old Testament have nothing but a fearful day of judgment to look forward to. That would be bad news, friend. The good news, the gospel, is that Jesus did come to save. We all need to be forgiven. If we refuse His grace, then we'll spend eternity apart from God, largely because of our pride.[11] Author Elyse Fitzpatrick writes in her fantastic book, *Found in Him*:

> "Jesus did not come to earth to be our example. He did
> not come to be our life coach, psychologist, mentor or
> cheerleader. He came to be our redeemer and to bear all
> the weight of the wrath we deserve. He came to die, and
> in so doing to glorify His Father by standing with us."[12]

RESCUED BY GOD'S GRACE THROUGH FAITH

One of my good friends spent some time in the Mississippi state correctional system. Shortly after arriving there, he came to understand the gospel in a life-altering way and became a Christian. His conversion was so radical that he began speaking to other inmates about it—first in small groups, and then in crowds. After a while, he was given the opportunity to travel to other institutions to share his story of meeting Jesus and receiving forgiveness for his sins. After years of genuine service to other inmates, it was clear that his wasn't your typical jailhouse conversion. One day, the governor's office notified him that he had been offered clemency for his crimes. He would not have to serve the balance of his sentence. What a relief that must have been.

However, imagine him sitting in his small cell, thinking about what it meant to his pride to admit that he was wrong and needed a pardon from the state in order to be free. Imagine him refusing what was freely offered to him. The offer of forgiveness and saving grace is genuinely held out to all. Unfortunately, unless a person is able to admit their need for Jesus's redemption, they'll continue in bondage for eternity and pay the penalty for those sins on their own.

Perhaps you're skeptical that all it takes is humility before God to be rescued from your sins. You wouldn't be alone, as I've been told that *my* understanding of Christianity is too good to be true. "A free gift from God? Forgiveness was granted because Jesus took my place? Unearned right to be one of His children?" I'll say this: Yes, IF it weren't true, it WOULD be too good to be true. One reason that God's unconditional love and grace are difficult to comprehend is that unearned favor is a rarity. On our best day, we wish we loved others unconditionally, but we often fail.

By contrast, God's gifts are given by His grace. His love is unconditional. When we humble ourselves before Him and genuinely ask for divine mercy through Christ's sacrifice, He forgives our sin (mercy) and gives us what we don't deserve. Grace (unmerited blessing) is not about avoiding the punishment we deserve. It is about getting the reward we don't deserve. In Christ, we're forgiven for our past and present sins through His willingness to be punished in our place. But we are also forgiven for sins we've yet to commit. Jesus died for all our transgressions. We look back to 2,000 years ago, when Jesus hung on the cross, but He was actually looking *forward* and paying for all the future sins of those who would look to Him.[13]

Our finite minds struggle to grasp that God in the flesh (Jesus Christ) died for all of our current and future sins. This lack of comprehension makes some of us insecure and frightened about our eternal destiny. It's as if we think we have to confess every misdeed before we die to ensure we'll spend eternity with God. If we've begun a heartfelt relationship with God (by His grace and through our faith), all of our sins are forgiven, and we can rest. Scripture says that if we confess with our mouth that Jesus is Lord and believe in our heart that God raised Him from the dead, we can rest easy because we are rescued.[14]

Seeing and experiencing God's grace in Christ is a must if you ever expect to be able to trust Him enough to not lose sight of the path, especially when it is so tempting to venture off on your own and lose your way. The first key to keeping the path in sight is understanding it theologically. If we're not clear about why we are confident in the presence of God, then it's unlikely our hearts will overflow with love for Him. It's also doubtful that we'll be able to discern when someone tries to convince us that our path is either the wrong one or only one of a number of possible paths to God.

THE HOLY SPIRIT AND NEW BIRTH

The issue of whether or not a person is "saved" by their faith alone or whether it is a combination of faith and works has been a hotly debated topic since the Christian church's inception in the first century. We've already shown how the Council of Nicaea formulated the Nicene Creed to refute the heresy of Arius's false teaching about Jesus. The concern of the bishops and the newly converted Emperor Constantine was personal and national peace. However, the answer to the question "Is a person saved and redeemed by God as a result of their faith alone?" was answered by the first church council. As a result of the Jerusalem Council, detailed in Acts 15, we can clearly conclude that a person becomes a Christian by virtue of their faith alone. The issue for that time was whether or not a person had to be circumcised in addition to calling out in faith to Jesus for salvation. Some contentious people believed so. The apostle Peter had heard and seen differently from the Holy Spirit, who'd lived in his soul since Pentecost.

This much is clear from Scripture: To be a Christian, a person must have God's Holy Spirit living within them. The concept of "rebirth" by the Holy Spirit is discussed many places in the Scripture. In response to a specific question about whether or not a person can have eternal life, Jesus responded that a person must born of the Holy Spirit.[15] On the night that He was betrayed to His death, Jesus taught that when He was resurrected the Holy Spirit would come to live in His followers.[16] We see this new phenomenon of the Spirit living inside of people demonstrated on Pentecost. According to Acts, God's plan was to help everyone in attendance at the annual Jewish Pentecost festival recognize the new era that had dawned. Not only did God intend to demonstrate the truth about Jesus's being resurrected, but He also wanted people to see that the Holy Spirit was now living inside of people.[17]

Jesus's disciples had come out of hiding and had been "baptized" or born of the Spirit. As a demonstration of the Spirit's presence, each disciple prayed aloud in the languages of the different people groups present, even though these disciples previously knew only their own language. The Scriptures say that when the Spirit came to live inside the disciples, they saw "tongues of fire" coming to rest on them. This is reminiscent of what happened to the Hebrew people when they were traveling across the Sinai desert after being freed from bondage in Egypt. God instructed Moses to create a tent of meeting (mobile tabernacle) where His presence would come to live in the middle of the people as they camped. When the Spirit came to reside in the tabernacle, there was a powerful display of power.[18]

> "**Seeing and experiencing God's grace in Christ is a must if you ever expect to be able to trust Him enough to not lose sight of the path, especially when it is so tempting to venture off on your own and lose your way.**"

Fast-forward from Israel's trek through Sinai, past the day of Pentecost mentioned in Acts 2, and up to the first church council in recorded history. The Council in Jerusalem (Acts 15) concluded that the Gentiles did not have to be circumcised in order to be Christians. A group of Jewish converts had been stating that in addition to believing that Jesus had died for their sins, Gentiles would also need to be circumcised, and understandably, this was creating a church crisis in Pisidian Antioch. Remember, getting circumcised as an adult in the first century was no small commitment (think flint rocks and no pain medication). More importantly, the addition of one single act made salvation not the product of what Jesus had done, but ultimately whatever action was added to that faith. This threatens how secure a Christian can feel about their relationship with God, and it dims Christ's glory and opens the door of pride to the person who acts correctly.

Acts records that Peter speaks and brings the discussion to an end. In Peter's previous experiences, God directed him to travel and speak to a Roman centurion and a group of Gentiles in Caesarea. Much to Peter's surprise, the Holy Spirit came upon these non-Jews just as He did for the Jews on Pentecost. God let the apostles know that the Spirit was not living only in Jewish hearts, but in ALL human hearts.

> "After much discussion, Peter got up and addressed them: 'Brothers, you know that some time ago God made a choice among you that the Gentiles might hear from my lips the message of the gospel and believe. God, who knows the heart, showed that he accepted them by giving the Holy Spirit to them, just as he did to us. He did not discriminate between us and them, for he purified their hearts by faith. Now then, why do you try to test God by putting on the necks of Gentiles a yoke that neither we nor our ancestors have been able to bear? No! We believe it is through the grace of our Lord Jesus that we are saved, just as they are.'"
>
> **Acts 15:7-11**

Peter's words shout from the Council of Jerusalem that a person is saved by grace alone through faith alone. That grace was evident when the Holy Spirit came to live in believers, which happens when they called out to God for mercy and He *"purified their hearts by faith"* through the perfect blood sacrifice of His Son, Jesus. Having been cleansed by Christ's sacrifice, believers were a spotless temple where God's Holy Spirit could live. That's why the fourth-century Council of Nicaea reaffirmed, "We believe in the Holy Spirit, the Lord, the giver of life, who proceeds from the Father [and the Son], who with the Father and the Son is worshiped and glorified, who has spoken through the prophets." As Peter said to the Council in Jerusalem, once we have the Holy Spirit, we are Christians. Once we are Christians, it would be illogical to think we would have to do anything else to become one or stay one. We are saved by God's grace, through our faith alone, evidenced by the Holy Spirit's presence in us.

SPIRITUAL LASIK SURGERY

Not long ago I finally went in for laser surgery to correct my nearsightedness. I didn't know that when they reshape your cornea to correct this problem, it can hamper your ability to see things up-close. Unfortunately, my first LASIK surgery resulted in my not being able to see anything. Something was amiss with the equipment or the technician. I was unable to see far away or close-up. Fortunately, I have thick corneas. They were able to do the surgery again and accurately set my vision, which is now better than 20/20.

For 2,000 years, hundreds of millions of Christians have viewed their lives and the world around them through the lens that Jesus Christ is God in the flesh. Believers have contended that this humble carpenter from Nazareth mirrored the attributes of God perfectly because He was divine by nature. If Jesus was the exact representation of the Father's being, weary souls could come to Him and rest, knowing that He compassionately sees us as bruised reeds that He wouldn't break.[19] The Scriptures and the church testify to a God that is visible in Christ and is more patient and gracious than we dream. People without Christ might fancy this depiction of God, but without any evidence to support that portrayal, how would they know? Through Jesus we have been given proof that we weren't foolishly optimistic about God being long-suffering and kind. And His resurrection from the dead proves that we're not just thinking wishfully.

According to Scripture, to have a relationship with God, you simply need to humbly acknowledge your need for His mercy and grace—and sincerely desire to turn from your current life path and follow the risen Christ. However, for all this to be authentic, Jesus needed to physically rise from His grave. The Nicene Creed says that "on the third day he rose again in accordance with the Scriptures; he ascended into heaven and is seated at the right hand of the Father." If that's not true, then we have been duped. We have been falsely led to believe that God's character could be seen in the person of Jesus because He was God in the flesh.

This is why the Resurrection is another one of those Jenga pieces that makes or breaks real Christianity. If Jesus didn't rise from the dead, then He is a liar who told His disciples and all who could hear Him that He would do so.[20] And if He lied, Jesus would be a sinner—and no longer an innocent sacrifice for others. If Jesus's disciples stole His body and buried it in the desert, they are all conspirators who perpetrated a fraud on foolish humanity. What they testify to in the Scriptures is a lie not to be trusted. If Jesus was not truly God in human flesh, we have no substantial proof that Almighty God is anywhere nearly as gracious as Jesus was. Scripture says that Jesus is the exact representation of God's being.[21] This is the value of gospel clarity; it deepens our spiritual confidence.

The good news is that Jesus did rise from the dead. All but one of the original twelve disciples died proclaiming this to be true, and no one dies for a lie that they manufactured, especially if they've not personally benefited from the resulting conspiracy to deceive. Clarity in our beliefs about Christ is critical to both our enjoyment of our faith and our endurance in pursuing intimacy with the Lord. Who Jesus was is supremely important to the Christian understanding of spiritual life. If Jesus wasn't God, He wasn't perfect. If He wasn't perfect, He couldn't be a perfect sacrifice for our sins. If Jesus didn't rise from the dead and ascend to His throne at the right hand of the Father, He's in no position to be your mediator or listen to your worship.

If Jesus didn't present His blood to God in the throne room of heaven as a sacrifice for our sins, you and I are left with the fearful prospect of facing a just God. We can hope we're morally good enough to make the cut, but for those of us who know we're selfish and broken, there is little hope for peace based on our good thoughts and deeds. The gospel is that Jesus has done this for us. Jesus fully atoned for our sins by taking the guilt and punishment for them, so we can be completely at peace with our Father, restored to the intimate proximity for which we were created. The Holy Spirit now resides in the human temple of every believer in Jesus.

This brings us to the two important questions I asked when I first believed the gospel: 1. How do I know the Holy Spirit lives in me? 2. If I believe that I am securely in friendship with God for eternity, what's to keep me from disregarding what His Word says about how I should live? Presuming we have gospel clarity about the message of Christianity, we should focus on what should motivate us to obey the Lord's commands.

EIGHT.

The Motive of Love

After a few years of being married, you learn important things about your spouse. In my case, it took me a while to learn that if I spoke her "love language" of service (meaning I cleaned up the house without her having to ask), she was receptive to just about anything I suggested. Yet, it would seem wrong if I took advantage of what she thinks is an effort to love her and used it to my own ends. Let's say I want a huge new flat-screen television for my man cave, but we've agreed to talk about purchases that exceed a certain dollar amount. I then hatch a plan: While she's at work, I will mow the yard, clean the garage, make the bed, do the dishes, and clean up the living room.

I expect she will come home and be elated that I, seemingly, communicated my love for her through service. After ordering dinner so she won't have to worry about cooking anything, I plan to pop the question: "What do you think about getting a new TV for my man cave?" This would violate the trust in our relationship. Jesus teaches that love is giving sacrificially without expecting anything in return. Mixed motives tend to expose our lack of love for others. In this scenario, my wife might be happy that the house was clean, but when she inevitably realized that I didn't do it out of love, she would be disappointed in me.

FAITH AND WORKS

We concluded the previous chapter by asking a couple of questions that face us if view a relationship with God as a free gift. We might ask, "How do I know the Holy Spirit lives in me?" and "If I know I'm eternally secure in Christ, what will motivate me to obey Scripture's countercultural and counterintuitive commands?" The answer to both of these questions is connected to the relationship between our salvation and good works. Historically, churches have been concerned that if parishioners were certain they were going to heaven, they would cease fearing God, and disobey Him at will.

This discussion usually revolves around the previously mentioned teaching from the apostle James. In his letter to the church, James declares that a faith without works is dead. He says that demons believe in God, so the test of genuine faith is if it produces good works.[1] James 1:27 states, "Religion that God our Father accepts as pure and faultless is this: to look after orphans and widows in their distress and to keep oneself from being polluted by the world." This one-two punch from James has led some to conclude that eternal salvation is a product of faith in Jesus (simple belief) plus an ambiguous number of good works.

I have a threefold concern about the notion that one's friendship with God depends on good works. First, the uncertainty of our eternal destiny would create great anxiety and terror, resulting in despair because we can never know if we've done enough good things. An honest assessment of the good works we haven't done would make most conclude that there is not much hope in totaling our good and bad deeds. This also presumes that we know all of the bad things we've done. Truth be told, we're pretty callous and often need others to point out how we've sinned against them.

Second, a friendship with God that's based on good works can negatively affect relationships, which require humility. Requiring good works to be secure in one's relationship with God creates a significant temptation to boast of our goodness in comparison to others. Additionally, if our own misdeeds were met with harsh, merciless, judgment from self-righteous believers, it would make us less likely to confess our sins to one another (which James also tells us to do).[2] It certainly would keep us from humbling ourselves when confronted by others about our bad behavior. Pride and fear make us defensive, which is a toxic combination in a church. My encounters with ex-church people has taught me that this toxicity is one chief reason they leave the faith of their youth.

Third, contending that good works are part of the formula that determines our eternal destiny creates mixed motives for obeying God's commands. It could make us feel that God is somehow in our debt. Just as my "good deeds" for my wife had an ulterior motive, "serving" God so He won't throw you into hell is a self-interested reason for complying with His commands. Loving (giving without expecting anything in return) becomes impossible in a relationship fraught with insecurity. Under these conditions, uncertainty and fear will be what others recognize about our religious experiences and expressions.

ARE WORKS PART OF THE EQUATION?

Over the years, I've tried to clarify the gospel by defining religious systems in terms of mathematical equations. My dad was a math teacher before becoming a union executive, so the arithmetic apple apparently doesn't fall far from the tree. Here are my four categories of religious systems:

(1) Our Good Works = Our Secure Relationship with God

In this system, we strive to become better people so that we will be acceptable to God. We perform good works for others and follow our religious system's rules or creeds. Our efforts are designed to win God's favor, in this life or the next. Many ancient religions believed that by good works or personal sacrifice, human beings could appease God's wrath. Almost every religion is some form of the equation "Good works = Our Secure Relationship with God."

(2) Our Existence = Our Secure Relationship with God

In this system, God exists, and humankind is fallible and incapable of being perfect. However, God intends to forgive everyone. It is often referred to as "universalism" because God will forgive everyone in the universe, regardless of their wrongdoings or lack of remorse for them. This salvation will happen regardless of one's moral performance on this planet or what they believe about God. Some universalists believe that "bad" people won't be punished forever; they'll just cease to exist, which I can testify would barely qualify as a deterrent to my bad behavior. You can think of this religious system in terms of the equation "Existence = Our Secure Relationship with God."

(3) Simplistic Belief in Jesus = Our Secure Relationship with God

This system, sometimes called "easy faith," is held by some Christian-identified people. In some ways its merely a Christian culture version of system two. These folks either choose to ignore what Scripture says about Christian living, or unknowingly don't think that God has any expectations of our interactions with Him or how we live. Some use this mischaracterization of biblical Christianity to sin against God and others. My experience has been that people in this category often resent anyone pointing them to Scripture's dictates about loving God or our neighbors. Simplistic Belief in Jesus = Secure Relationship with God.

(4) Faith (Reliance on Christ's Work) = Our Secure Relationship with God + Works

The fourth system is what orthodox or biblical Christianity claims Jesus came to do. Perfection is demanded if we want to be in God's holy presence. And God demands justice for sins committed against His holiness. However, as broken humanity, we're incapable of perfection and deserve to be punished for our evil deeds. Because we're imperfect and can't atone for our own misdeeds, our heavenly Father solves the predicament by sending His only begotten Son to do that for us. Good works are a part of this system of doctrine, but they are intrinsically connected to salvation and the necessary evidence of genuine faith.

Jesus provides "salvation" for us in two senses. First, by being punished for the sins of all who will trust in Him, He provides forgiveness. Second, by perfectly obeying the law during His earthly journey, Jesus fulfilled the law on our behalf and now we confidently know he can sympathize with our struggle. On the cross, He exchanged His goodness for our sin to bring us to God.[3] Theologians refer to this doctrine as imputation (being credited with Christ's righteousness).[4]

SO, WHAT'S THE DIFFERENCE?

There are significant differences between system four (historic Christianity) and the first three. In the first system, even if we assume one could live a "good enough" life to avoid making any big blunders or overtly hurting anyone, perfection isn't possible. So, there is no way of knowing until the dreaded "Judgment Day" if a person is right with God. And if someone could perform religious duties ably enough, they would be the one credited for their salvation. They would inevitably fall prey to self-righteousness. In their pride, they will credit themselves with enough goodness and well-intentioned behavior to "force" God's hand to allow them into His presence. God would be obliged to allow their safe passage into a pleasant afterlife. Humans are the center of this religion and the ones who receive the credit for good works.

In system two, humankind can act unjustly, and there is no eternal system of justice or punishment—regardless of how cruel, evil, or horrifying the behavior on this earth. The monsters of history, the Roman Emperor Nero, Attila the Hun, Genghis Khan, Adolph Hitler, and everyone before and after them are all free from any eternal divine justice. God, if He exists at all, will simply look the other way and say, "I forgive you." There is no requirement of saving faith, good works, or acknowledging one's wrongdoings. Either there is no judgment or the judgment is our ceasing to exist for eternity (which technically could be called a judgment).

In this system, God, if He exists, is unjust. The good news is that in the person of Jesus Christ is this dilemma of mercy and justice solved. The apostle Paul wrote that through Jesus Christ, God is able to be just (Jesus satisfies God's holy requirement for the punishment of sins) and able to be merciful (we are spared the punishment we deserve).[5]

The third system is a cultural phenomenon. In some places there is a social benefit to being identified as a Christian. As a result, there are many who will declare that they're Christians, but have an unbiblical definition of what it means to be a Christ follower.

For them, Jesus is eternal fire insurance for anyone who simply acknowledges they believe in Him, no matter how insincere their profession of faith is. They have no intention of following Him, and they incorrectly presume that providing "get out of hell free cards" is all Jesus came to accomplish.

ARE GOOD WORKS REQUIRED?

Advocates of salvation by faith alone have long been accused of saying that works are not part of our equation (Faith = Salvation). However, that is not true. Scripture says that the works of salvation are part of God's requirement for His children, as evidenced by Ephesians 2:8-10. That passage states clearly that we're saved by grace, through faith, "not by works so no one can boast." But verse ten punctuates the importance of the good works that God requires: "For we are God's handiwork, created in Christ Jesus to do good works, which God prepared in advance for us to do."

This is where the question about our motive for obedience (what makes us obey if we're secure in our eternal destiny) intersects with our curiosity about whether or not the Holy Spirit genuinely lives in us. Scripture teaches that the Holy Spirit is a person, not an impersonal force. He is the third person of the triune God and is sent by the Father and the Son to be present with us and live in us. Jesus said:

> "If you love me, keep my commands. And I will ask the Father, and he will give you another advocate to help you and be with you forever—the Spirit of truth. The world cannot accept him, because it neither sees him nor knows him. But you know him, for he lives with you and will be in you."
> **John 14:15-17**

Being a Christian is not about acquiring fire insurance to avoid eternal hell. It is about restoring God's world to its original intention: revealing His glory in us and in creation. Step one in this process is God's redeeming the focal point of His creation, His beloved children. Restoring our fellowship with God is the starting point for the remainder of Christ's kingdom work. With the intimate presence of the Holy Spirit literally within us, and our spiritual strength being deepened by gospel clarity, we are motivated by three realities.

First, obedience is how we show our love for God. In fellowship with Him, we grow in our love for Him, serving with gladness in light of His glorious grace. Second, His commands (while at times counterintuitive and countercultural) are good for us. We were created to operate in harmony with God's character. It is significant that Adam and Eve were tempted with the words, "Did God really say?"[6] Our enemy's goal has always been to tempt humanity to question the trustworthiness of God's Word. Third, God is our creator and is due our reverence, worship, and obedience. He may be our Father, but He's also our glorious King. We follow Jesus so that His character and attributes can be seen in our actions. For instance, our obedience proclaims God's love, which is why the church's care for society's marginalized is so vital to its missional success.[7]

The Heidelberg Catechism was written in 1563 by church reformers in Germany. Question #86 of that catechism asks, "Since we have been delivered from our misery by grace through Christ without any merit of our own, why then should we do good works?" The answer is a terrific summary of why we should obey God: "Because Christ, having redeemed us by his blood, is also restoring us by his Spirit into his image, so that with our whole lives we may show that we are thankful to God for his benefits, so that he may be praised through us, so that we may be assured of our faith by its fruits, and so that by our godly living our neighbors may be won over to Christ." Obedience is our response to His grace and goodness. It is an act of gratitude to and love for God. Our desire to do such things assures us that God has genuinely converted us. Our disposition has been changed, and while we will never obey perfectly in this life, we long to do so.

The New Testament gives clarity about the reasons NOT to do good works. We don't do good works to earn our salvation. Only through Christ's works is redemption and restoration to fellowship with God possible. We don't obey to "keep" our salvation, which would be another form of salvation by good works. Finally, we are not to be motivated to serve to make ourselves look good to people or feel better about ourselves. These drives are inherently selfish. However, my longing to more faithfully follow Jesus sometimes has more to do with feeling better about my status before God than anything else. I teach and believe that I'm unconditionally loved by Him because of the gift of Christ's righteousness, but I still long to feel entitled to be in God's presence because of my impressive behavior. This is a futile pursuit because I will never find real security in my track record of loving God and others. Author Jerry Bridges wrote:

> "Our good works are not truly good unless they are motivated by a love for God and a desire to glorify Him. But we cannot have such a God-ward motivation if we think we must earn God's favor by our obedience or if we fear we may forfeit God's favor by our disobedience. Such a works-oriented motivation is essentially self-serving; it is prompted more by what we think we can gain or lose from God than by a grateful response to the grace He has already given us through Jesus Christ."[8]

You may ask, "Do motives matter if good is being accomplished?" To go back to my earlier example, my wife is always happy when the house is clean. But she wouldn't call my ulterior-motivated act of cleaning the house "love" for her. It's the same with God. Does He work through mixed motives? Sure. As a minister, I have battled with why I'm doing what I do. Hopefully, most of it was for God and to serve people. But, as I've stated, my own honor and sense of value have often motivated me to do just about everything in my life.

I believe God is happy when justice is done, and mercy is extended to the marginalized and needy. However, one side effect of selfishness driving our service to God and others is that we risk becoming self-righteous about our altruism, and judgmental of others whose zeal doesn't match ours. I've seen this among people who are zealous about mercy and justice—and in church cultures where certain Christian virtues are extolled over the others. In these places, an emphasis on one aspect of God's holiness, the church's mission, or extra-biblical cultural expectations masks the shortcomings of the church and its leaders.

THE FRUIT OF THE SPIRIT AND THE LORDSHIP OF JESUS

In my backyard, I have two trees: one lime and one lemon. They are both the same age, but the lime tree is overflowing with fruit. The lemon tree has produced a grand total of one lemon. One. You might think that something is wrong with the tree. I did too, until my wife and I considered how the trees are situated. The lime tree is positioned just off the bottom corner of the sloped concrete patio. Whenever it rains or our sprinklers have runoff onto the deck, much of the water drains down toward the lime tree. The lemon tree is perched above the backyard on a sloped hill. At first, we didn't realize the disadvantaged position that Mr. Lemon occupies. No extra water flows his way, and erosion of the hill has exposed his young roots. Eventually, I built a box to hold the dirt around the base of the tree, but it's still produced only one lemon.

Speaking of the evidence of the Holy Spirit in His followers' lives, Jesus said we would "produce fruit." His apostles also talked about the "fruits of the Holy Spirit."[9] The first century's agrarian culture inspired Jesus to craft metaphors and parables about farms, animals, and crops.

We may ask ourselves, "How do we know the Holy Spirit lives in us?" We see the evidence of His presence manifest itself in how we live, what we think, and what we say. Jesus declared, "The mouth speaks what the heart is full of."[10] In the Sermon on the

Mount, Jesus warned:

> "Watch out for false prophets. They come to you in sheep's clothing, but inwardly they are ferocious wolves. By their fruit you will recognize them. Do people pick grapes from thornbushes, or figs from thistles? Likewise, every good tree bears good fruit, but a bad tree bears bad fruit. A good tree cannot bear bad fruit, and a bad tree cannot bear good fruit. Every tree that does not bear good fruit is cut down and thrown into the fire. Thus, by their fruit you will recognize them."
> **Matthew 7:15-20**

Like the two trees in my backyard, authentic Christians produce fruit in differing volumes and varying paces, for various reasons. Sometimes, preexisting conditions make it more challenging for some to display the fruit of the Spirit compared to others. If we were raised in a loving Christian home, we have a head start. If we didn't suffer abuse or trauma in our childhood, we won't carry some of the emotional burdens that others might. All of these factors play a role in how quickly we reflect the character of Christ.

> **" Scripture assures us that although Jesus never sinned, He understands the difficulty associated with obeying the Father's will, and He is empathetic".**

Gaining gospel clarity in this area of our spiritual lives means that we begin to see that God is more patient with us than some churches and church leaders may have led us to believe. Because some are afraid that God's patience provides a license to sin at will, they assign themselves the duty of assessing the volume of "fruit production" in our character. Ironically, impatient and unkind Christians who judge you for not producing the fruit quickly enough are not demonstrating the Spirit fruits of patience or kindness. Scripture assures us that although

Jesus never sinned, He understands the difficulty associated with obeying the Father's will, and He is empathetic.[11]

Recognizing that criticizing others unsympathetically is part of human nature, Jesus used another farm image in a parable about judgmentalism. He told the story of a man who sowed good seed in his field. In the middle of the night, an enemy came and sowed weeds among the wheat. Later that season, when the wheat sprouted and formed heads, the weeds appeared too. The workers asked where the weeds came from, and if they should pull them. The owner replied, "No, because while you are pulling the weeds, you may uproot the wheat with them. Let both grow together until the harvest." The farmer knew that in the early stages of growth, if you're too quick to eliminate what you view as a problem, you may damage your good crops.[12]

The parable should keep us from judging one another. Its intent is echoed in other apostolic writings, where we are urged to "be completely humble and gentle; be patient, bearing with one another in love." Unfortunately, many Christians have suffered at the hands of brothers and sisters who deem some sins less egregious than others. In my lifetime, there has been no greater example of this than how the church has treated people in the LGBTQ community. The 1980s televangelist Jimmy Swaggart once preached that homosexuality might be the worst sin. To my shame, I confess that when I was a young Christian, I bought this perspective about human sexuality, believing that my sexual disobedience to Scripture was not as bad as those of gay-identified men and women. This type of arrogance has alienated many people from Christianity.

Perhaps we feel that way about our own sin in general, but same-sex attracted Christians have felt an alienation, because they often feel they have to hide their inner struggle in ways that others don't. As a youth pastor in a different era, I spoke insensitively and crassly about the LGBTQ struggle to counterintuitively follow Scripture's teaching about human sexuality. This type of thoughtlessness and pride is part of the reason why many gay-identified Christians have decided that they don't want to be in theologically orthodox churches. One way that gospel clarity strengthens us is by deepening our empathy for fellow believers who are struggling against sin as we are.

DOOMED TO REPEAT HISTORY

Philosopher George Santayana declared that those who cannot remember the past are condemned to repeat it. One thing we can learn from our historical struggle against sin is that hiding in shame doesn't produce a change of heart. For a time, a person can be silenced into compliance and hide their private battle. But unless there is an inward desire to behave differently, the behavior will, at best, go underground for a season. And yet we continue in pointless self-flagellation to make us obey God's law, with little concern about our motives. Compliance to the law without love or need for Jesus is the way of the pharisee.

Our hearts change when we see God's love. Gospel clarity about our motivation for obeying God is critical for our success in growing in Christlikeness. If we aren't motivated by a growing comprehension of God's love for us, we won't love Him. To grow in our love for God, we must increase our knowledge of Scripture's assurances of His love for us in Christ. Shame may create behavioral change in the short term, but it will not produce a change in one's attitude and actions unless we feel secure in our status as God's children.

> "Those who cannot remember the past are condemned to repeat it."—George Santayana

If we know anything from history, it's that people won't be bullied into moral compliance. Not by law or by society. To avoid cultural isolation, people may keep their inclinations to themselves, but internally they'll seethe with anger and prepare for retribution. If modern political movements seek to effect change without any corresponding grace, their enemies might comply on the surface, but underground movements will likely grow and then boomerang back into the world with a vengeance.

What produces change in us? We need more of the approach that Jesus took. John 1:14 said of Christ, "*The Word became flesh and made his dwelling among us. We have seen his glory, the glory of the one and only Son, who came from the Father, full of grace and truth.*" We need a renewal of the twin pillars of grace and truth. We need the truth about what our bad behavior does to us and others, coupled with patience for one another, which humbly demonstrates how God has been exceedingly patient with us.

In my years as a pastor, I have seen different generations grow impatient with Christ's bride (the church) for different reasons. In the 1970s, the charismatic church came forth from the Jesus movement and correctly showed the church that it often ignored the power of the Spirit. In the 1980s, the seeker-sensitive movement pushed the church to engage the unchurched as it hadn't previously. In the 1990s, the theologically Reformed church challenged the theological depth of the church at large.

In this century, the dominant corrective movement is that of social justice. All of these movements have correctly pointed out various sins and flaws of the church. Real repentance and change are required by the church when it has erred or sinned. However, as these movements become more mainstream, segments of these corrective revivals feel entitled to ignore the biblical command to be humble and patient with one another. This unbridled self-righteousness hinders the pace of change because it is out of step with the spirit of Jesus, which is gracious and truthful.

Christians of every stripe must commit to humbly removing the plank from our own eyes before reaching for the speck in another's. By being impatient with those who aren't as mature as we think we are, we fail to motivate people through gracious truth, but rather through frustrated condescension. As a student pastor in the 1990s, I was zealous about evangelism because it was my calling and because I recognized that churches had grown lethargic about sharing the good news. From my vantage point, conservative white evangelical churches were spending too much money building buildings and marching for conservative political causes.

I believed (and still do) that making friends with those who need to experience God's love through us is a high priority, one that is specifically commanded in Scripture. I grew frustrated and impatient with our church's adult ministries, and I demonstrated an ungodly level of self-righteous indignation about what I perceived as a passive attitude toward reaching nonbelievers. I had to apologize to some of those I hurt. Sometimes preachers, prophets, and proclaimers of truth hurt people in a rush to announce their message. As Christians, we're called to stop and say I'm sorry.

A JEHOVAH'S WITNESS'S WORST NIGHTMARE

When I was a seminary student, I had a study partner who now has been one of my best friends for decades. One afternoon we were studying for an exam in our New Testament class. As we worked on memorizing the first chapter of the Gospel of John, we were discussing the linguistic implications of what that chapter says about Jesus: "In the beginning was the Word, and the Word was with God, and the Word was God."[11] The "Word" John references is Jesus (which becomes clearer later in the chapter), and in this verse he clearly states that Word was not only with God in the beginning, but He was God. We discussed in Chapter Seven the important implications of Jesus's being eternally one with the Father, God from God. Our salvation and our confidence in God's love rest on Jesus's divinity.

As my buddy and I were talking this through, someone knocked at the door. A Jehovah's Witness door-to-door evangelist was wanting to visit about her religion. This middle-aged woman was obviously doing her best to comply with the expectations of her religion, which has been deemed a cult by orthodox Christianity. (Jehovah's Witnesses are considered non-orthodox and not Christian because they deny Jesus's divinity. Like the Arians of the third and fourth centuries, Jehovah's Witnesses deny that Jesus was eternally begotten of the Father.

What makes this encounter particularly interesting is that this group's translation of the New Testament changes the first verse of John's Gospel by a single word. By inserting the letter "a" into the last part of the verse, their version of John 1:1 reads, "In the beginning was the Word, and the Word was with God, and the Word was a (my emphasis) God." They do this because they think that Jesus was a human being with no divine nature. By translating the verse saying Jesus was "a god," He then can be denied as the one true God. What are the odds that a JW door-to-door evangelist shows up at the apartment of two seminary students who know all of this information? That's a proselytizing nightmare.

She was not the first cult member I have talked with over the years. Some ride bikes around our neighborhood and city looking for people who might be interested in hearing about what they believe. I know from experience that if you speak with someone from these cults, you should be prepared to listen a fair bit. If you interrupt their packaged presentation, there is a good chance they'll start over, taking more of your time. My experience in talking to some religious proselytizers is that they have a hollow, glazed-over look. It's often like they're not talking to you but instead talking near you and about you. I've experienced this same phenomenon with people trying to get me to buy into their multilevel marketing business. One suspects that their efforts to tell others is more about their need than about others' needs. Cultists coming to our homes appear more concerned about checking off their religious duties than coming to our aid. To be fair, I've known some Christians who had a similar demeanor in their faith sharing. When I was a young believer this was unfortunately my tactless approach.

Yes, when your motives for obeying God are selfish, most people can tell. And God always knows. This is another reason I am so convinced that once a person is genuinely converted to Christianity, they can't ever stop being a Christian. Yes, some people have associated with Christianity but later denied any real belief or experience with Christ. But for the person who truly has God's Holy Spirit in their soul, they can't do (or fail to do) anything that would jeopardize their eternal destination. God wants us to be free to love and obey Him for the reasons He has prescribed: His glory, our good, and to show love for others.

The apostle John was arguably Jesus's best friend. While Peter was the leader of the gang, John referred to himself in the third person as "the one whom Jesus loved."[13] John was the lone disciple at the foot of the cross with Jesus's mother. While hanging on the cross, Jesus entrusted the care of Mary, His mother, to John. John knew Jesus loved him, and his response was to serve and love the Lord in return. It was an intimate relationship between friends, not one of moral obligation and half-hearted effort. This is what God is calling us to.

In his first apostolic letter, John wrote:

"Dear friends, let us love one another, for love comes from God. Everyone who loves has been born of God and knows God. Whoever does not love does not know God, because God is love. This is how God showed his love among us: He sent his one and only Son into the world that we might live through him. This is love: not that we loved God, but that he loved us and sent his Son as an atoning sacrifice for our sins."
1 John 4:7-10

These are the two parallel expectations for Christians: We are to experience God's love and then extend it to each other. Those who have been truly born of God (being indwelled by the Spirit, born of the Spirit, or born again)[14] love others, because God is love. We demonstrate God's glorious love through our actions with others. John punctuates this well-known Scripture by saying that this is how God showed His love for us: He sent Jesus to be an atoning sacrifice for our sins. We live through Jesus and love God because He first loved us. This is gospel clarity in our motives.

DON'T COME IN UNTIL YOU'RE CLEAN

Early in my Christian experience I heard a Pentecostal pastor use a discouraging analogy. It took me years to discover why. It took me even longer to get the thought from influencing my faith practice. He was preaching about entering God's presence, and he likened it to an experience with his mother. When he got dirty playing outside and wanted to come into the kitchen to get a snack, his mother would stand at the door and say, "Not until you get that mud off of your feet." This was how I was taught about God's accessibility to me while I still had sin in my life. As you can imagine, an honest person would realize they would never be able to enter God's presence.

When church people see and hear these confusing anecdotes or recognize the pride in their leader's heart as they imply that they have earned the right to approach the Lord, they despair that they are unable to measure up. Their leaders aren't measuring up either; they've conveniently categorized their sin and struggle as less greasy than ours. As a result, despondent, struggling believers contemplate leaving the church because they don't know what to do when they don't desire to love God (sometimes for a lengthy season). Do they have to wait until they feel enough love for God to come back to church? Do they have to manufacture tears to show they truly feel bad for not trusting God's Word? Is God angry with them because they're prone to wander into sin? The writer of the book of Hebrews declares this about Jesus as He sits on His throne:

> "For we do not have a high priest who is unable to empathize with our weaknesses, but we have one who has been tempted in every way, just as we are—yet he did not sin. Let us then approach God's throne of grace with confidence, so that we may receive mercy and find grace to help us in our time of need."
> **Hebrews 4:15-16**

Jesus is gracious and compassionate, slow to anger and full of love. His tenderness with struggling sinners is evident in the way He dealt with those who were at the bottom of the social ladder and often engulfed in sinful struggles. This is why the religious leaders of His day pejoratively referred to Jesus being a "friend of sinners."[15] As we grasp in more profound ways the security we have in Christ, our spiritual confidence grows. Our life in a broken world is a series of missteps followed by a series of apologies and recommitments to continue following. We never reach the summit in this lifetime. We're always climbing.

The 18th-century British hymn writer Joseph Hart penned these words to his classic, "Come Ye Sinners, Poor and Needy":

> **"Jesus is gracious and compassionate, slow to anger and full of love. His tenderness with struggling sinners is evident in the way He dealt with those who were at the bottom of the social ladder and often engulfed in sinful struggles."**

Come, ye sinners, poor and needy,
weak and wounded, sick and sore;
Jesus ready stands to save you,
full of pity, love, and power.

Come, ye weary, heavy laden,
lost and ruined by the fall;
if you tarry til you're better,
you will never come at all.

I will rise and go to Jesus!
He will save me from my sin.
By the riches of his merit,
there is joy and life in him.[16]

NINE.

The Mission of Christ

Why do we climb mountains? When I set out to hike to the top of Mount Wilson, I was sure of my purpose: climb to the peak and then hike back down. I would not have agreed to climb the mountain and stay there. Climbing a mountain is a two-part mission, unless you plan on dying along the way. This is the way of all things: marathon runners run in order to finish, fishers keep fishing in hopes of a good catch and then a return from sea, and couples begin a marriage they hope will last a lifetime. Most events sound one-dimensional, but they involve multiple aspects and components. The gospel is a lot like that.

We've looked at the need for clarity about the gospel message. To refine our vision of the gospel, I'll focus on the gospel mission. Some who promote the good news of grace in Christ resist saying there is more to the gospel mission than simply saving souls. In some cases, they emphasize a popular form of eschatology (study of the end times) that predicts the entire world will be destroyed at the consummation of history. With the understanding that "it's all gonna burn in the end," it's easy to see why adherents to this view don't bother trying to save the planet. For others, conflating the message of salvation in Christ with the mission of the church threatens the nature of salvation by faith alone. In this chapter, I hope to clarify the mission of the church, and in so doing, show the consistent theme of the gospel: God's grace always precedes the work of His people.

Jesus calls His gospel the "Gospel of the Kingdom," which sounds ominous to people afraid of theocratic governments. But Jesus's kingdom institutes changes to our world now, and into eternity. The gospel of Christ's kingdom, like His divinity, is composed of two parts that are inseparable and unified, but not to be mixed or confused.[1] Theologian Herman Ridderbos referred to the kingdom as containing the gift and the command. He said these two parts were the salvation that is proclaimed in Christ and the living out of that salvation in our world.[2]

With His coming to earth in Christ, God's rule has come to humanity in a unique way. Jesus intended for His followers to apply

His values so that His eternal kingdom would manifest itself on earth: "Your kingdom come, your will be done, on earth as it is in heaven."[3] That's how He taught us to pray. He wants His glory to be seen through the lives of His children from every nation, tribe, and tongue, as it will be in the future.[4] Our collective efforts here on earth should extend God's grace to all, so the world will see God's glory through Christ's body, the church.

I don't believe that Jesus saved us from our sins so that we could be the proverbial bystanders watching a building burn to the ground, while the overmatched firefighters battle to put out the blaze. As I mentioned in Chapter Four, the world is broken, and Jesus's restoration plan includes His glory being seen as His children shine the light of His presence into the world, producing godly change. Historically, we've seen theological tension between God's grace in salvation and the works that He commands us to do. We've explored this tension in the two previous chapters. But when it comes to the church's mission, the same debate continues between those who think that the church's mission is to "save sinners" and others who think it is "all about doing good works." Scripture says that it's both, but one follows the other.

> **" Our collective efforts here on earth should extend God's grace to all, so the world will see God's glory through Christ's body, the church."**

Some of the theological challenges center on semantics. My academic discipline is communications and rhetorical analysis, so I'm aware that certain groups say the same thing but use different nomenclature. Thus, they're unable to see the common ground. When power is the real agenda, humility and honest dialogue go by the wayside in favor of gaining advantage and winning. (I see this in pastoral marriage counseling too.) Having spent half of my ministry life in the American South, I regularly encountered conservative evangelicals and churches that openly conflated the Republican political agenda with God's kingdom work.

More recently, in the absence of any progressive social action in their church, some Christians are switching to congregations that talk about social justice every week. These churches sport an agenda that focuses almost exclusively on caring for the poor or engaging in justice actions. I believe caring for the needy and promoting justice are critical components of the church, but they aren't the only ones. Some Christians, having left theologically orthodox churches they assumed were too aligned with conservative politics (or simply neutral about politics), choose churches that are markedly different in their core belief systems. As I noted earlier, many of these people find that their new church communities don't respect their old beliefs.

This migration indicates that a church's social-justice activity can be seen as more important than theological clarity about how men and women enter into a life-changing relationship with God. Oddly, some of these churches have a one-sided view of the political process. One church that thinks conservative politics are the mission of the church, while another feels the same about liberal/progressive social action. What are we to think? Is political action the mission of the church? Is it part of the mission? How do we define which political actions best represent the church's mission?

LESSONS FROM BUILDING A CROSS

One thing I like about pastoring a small church is being involved in almost all of its activities. Megachurch ministers are usually specialists with a narrow focus about what they do for a large group of people. "Mini-church" pastors have to be jacks-of-all-trades for everyone in the congregation. For example, a staff member asked me to build a cross for creative use in our church. Fancying myself a handyman, I went to work. As I put this cross together, a couple things dawned on me. First, we don't build crosses anymore. We buy little ones, as fashion accessories, but building large crosses from wood is uncommon. Second, real wooden crosses aren't made with one piece. They're simply too big and oddly shaped to make a Roman-era cross from one piece of lumber.

Crosses in Jesus's time were made of two beams or logs. There was nothing artistic about them; they were torture devices. A Roman cross had a vertical beam that got dropped into a hole that was dug for stabilizing the apparatus. Before the cross was lifted, a horizontal crossbeam was attached to it. That horizontal beam was the one Jesus Christ carried up the Via Dolorosa in Jerusalem, as He made His way to the "Hill of the Skull" to be crucified.

They laid the crossbeam across the vertical beam and nailed those two pieces together. Then they used spikes to fix Jesus's hands and feet to the cross. Romans would drive the nails into the part of the hand where it connects to the wrist, so that the weight of the body wouldn't tear the hands away from the crossbeam. Then the cross, with the Savior on it, was dropped into place. Crucifixion was meant to be a long, painful death. Jesus's death was just that.

To illustrate the relationship between the gospel's work and its message, I use the cross of Jesus. It had two beams (dimensions), a vertical and a horizontal, but they were inseparable. In the same way, Jesus came to reconcile us to Himself (vertically), and to make us agents of reconciliation to the world (horizontally, in every way that the Scripture mandates us to be). A Roman cross was composed of two parts; so is the church's mission. We are to proclaim the good news that Jesus has come to reconcile people to Himself (vertical). We're also to proclaim that He brings good news to the poor and frees the oppressed (horizontal). It's not an either/or, but a both/and.

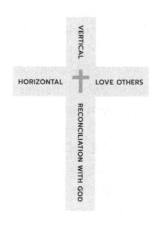

It's important to recognize that the weight of the horizontal beam is completely supported by the vertical beam. Without the vertical, the horizontal is nothing but a log on the ground. It is not a cross. The horizontal cannot and does not support the vertical. It lacks the power to do that. In the same way, the horizontal aspect of the gospel mission is completely supported by the vertical, not the other way around. The vertical is the priority—the most important aspect of the cross. Yes, a cross without a crossbeam is not a cross. It's a big pole in a hole. Faith without good works is not a real, living faith, as James has shown us. Religion that God accepts as pure and faultless is looking after orphans and widows in their distress, keeping oneself from being polluted by the world, and watching our words.[5]

Reducing the gospel to one dimension or the other robs it of its comprehensive nature and value. And conflating the gospel's two dimensions creates confusion, or worse, eliminates God's grace. When we don't prioritize God's redemptive grace, we fail to acknowledge that all of our works are a response to His love for us. God's grace and our faith in His redemptive work always precedes our good works.[6] Works are the necessary evidence of the gospel, but they are not how a person is made right before the Father. Reducing the gospel to "it's just about going to heaven" (which denies God's restoring His creation for His glory) or "it's just about good works on earth" (which denies that people must receive Jesus to have eternal life) doesn't paint an accurate picture of the gospel.

A CASE FOR THE HORIZONTAL

I have often heard enthusiastic and frustrated Christians ask, "Why can't we be like the first-century church? I want the church to be like it was in the book of Acts." I asked this as a young Christian. Now I realize that I hadn't read the fine print of that deal: You don't get first-century miracles without first-century problems. The fifth book of the New Testament, *The Acts of the Apostles*, is a historical account of the church's expansion from Jerusalem to Judea and Samaria and onward toward the ends of the earth. It records the Holy Spirit's miraculous power and the conversion of thousands of people to Christianity. But it also chronicles the persecution of the church, the killing of Christians for their profession of faith, and it details the church's internal conflicts. There were leadership divisions, theological controversies, and internal squabbling. This controversy often sprung from the historic cultural tension between the Jewish people and their newly embraced Gentile brothers and sisters in Christ.

Sometimes the conflict occurred within different subcultures of Jewish people. In Acts 6, we read of an early bump in the road: the growing pains of a church that went from a couple dozen people to thousands of new converts in a very short time.

In those days when the number of disciples was increasing, the Hellenistic Jews among them complained against the Hebraic Jews because their widows were being overlooked in the daily distribution of food. So the Twelve gathered all the disciples together and said, "It would not be right for us to neglect the ministry of the word of God in order to wait on tables. Brothers and sisters choose seven men from among you who are known to be full of the Spirit and wisdom. We will turn this responsibility over to them and will give our attention to prayer and the ministry of the word."
Acts 6:1-4

Having just begun the climb of faith, the church was already tripping over itself. If you want your church to be a "first-century" ministry, get ready for lots of conflict. Putting that many broken people together evokes the image of a cue ball breaking a freshly racked set of pool balls. In a church community, people are going to bounce off of one another, occasionally hurting one another (often unknowingly). Sometimes we miraculously end up where we hope to be. Usually, we discover again the truth of Jesus's words that we can do nothing without Him.[7] Such was the first-century church in Jerusalem.

It's worth noting some characteristics of that church. First, it attracted needy people who served others in need. Harvard religious professor Helmut Koester wrote that the early church was particularly welcoming to the marginalized:

> "Here is a community that invites you, which makes you an equal with all other members of that community. Which does not give you any disadvantages. On the contrary, it gives even the lowliest slave dignity and status. Moreover, the commandment of love is decisive. That is, the care for each other becomes very important. People are taken out of an isolation. If they are hungry, they know where to go. If they are sick, there is an elder who will lay on hands to them to heal them."[8]

Jesus's kingdom preaching was accentuated by works of mercy. God's mercy was reflected in the church's actions. The ultimate goal of extending mercy is for people to see God. Doing good things for people is not the end, but the wonderful means of portraying God's love and introducing Him to the world. Mercy should be a high priority for the church because it broadcasts the nature of the Savior.

Acts 6 also portrays the first church clash of cultures. The people distributing food to the poor were showing preference to the Hebraic Jews, but neglecting Hellenistic Jews. The first group of Jewish believers were from Judea and were culturally different from the second group, whose culture was rooted in Greek traditions and practices.

The church saw

"Doing good things for people is not the end, but the wonderful means of portraying God's love and introducing Him to the world. Mercy should be a high priority for the church because it broadcasts the nature of the Savior."

this prejudice as a direct threat to the gospel. Church leaders did not ignore this tension; they knew it endangered the church's witness. The Bible declares that no individual is more important to God than anyone else. And no one is made right with God by virtue of ethnicity, culture, or geography. Christianity proclaims that in Christ we are one race, but beautifully composed of different ethnicities. This is an important reality for Western Christians to understand, particularly my Caucasian brothers and sisters. Racism is an affront to the gospel because it communicates (louder than words) that one group is more important to God than another. The implication of this perceived favoritism has historically emboldened dominant ethnicities (such as the Hebraic Jews in Acts 6) to treat others as *lesser than*.

When ethnocentrism or racism invades the church, it contradicts the gospel by introducing pride. When an ethnic group believes their culture is better than others', they are communicating that they are more acceptable to God. When I was in seminary, I discussed contemporary forms of worship with a local pastor. His church had a highly liturgical worship style that featured classical music. This pastor's argument against contemporary forms of worship was that we should worship God with our very best. He contended that the best music ever created was European classical music. Hence, God should be worshiped only with classical music. Everything else was substandard. This is European culture-influenced ethnocentrism. It screams to those from different cultures and subcultures that people who don't worship in a High-Church, Eurocentric way are less acceptable to God. Or, at least, their worship is not as pleasing to God.

The early church emphasized caring for the poor and stamping out racial injustice, and they also prioritized teaching the good news of Christ's death and resurrection. The solution to the dilemma faced by a growing multiethnic church was for the apostles to appoint the women and men to choose qualified leaders to fill the role of "deacon" to lead service ministries. Acts 6:2 says that the apostles decided, "It would not be right for us to neglect the ministry of the word of God."

After establishing this team of leaders, the Word of God spread as never before.[9]

There is a reason for the primacy of gospel proclamation, which serves as the fountain from which all of this mercy and justice flows. As I've said, God's reconciling people through Jesus secures our vertical relationship with Him. Without the understanding that God sees everyone equal in their spiritual condition before Him (as sinners in need of a Savior), the church wouldn't have been able to acknowledge that the Gentiles or Hellenistic Jews were their complete equals. Knowing that we are saved by grace alone and that we're every bit as broken as the next person keeps us humble before everyone.

Prioritizing the proclamation of the gospel doesn't mean that the mercy and outreach of the church are less important. It means that people can't become fully devoted followers of Jesus until they first meet Him. People of privilege are unlikely to divest themselves of their status and stuff unless they acknowledge how they have been made right with God. Some conservative theologians raise concerns about conflating the gospel's redemptive message with its works. I share that concern, and I have aimed to dispel this worry. I believe the relationship between faith and works must be clearly defined both individually and corporately, especially during seasons when the church experiences correction.

THE CASE FOR THE VERTICAL

In Acts 1:8, Jesus says that His followers were going to be witnesses in their city (Jerusalem), their local region (Judea), and neighboring region (Samaria), and then throughout the world. If that was the only commission the church had received, we might conclude that the mission was simply to tell people about Jesus so they would become Christians, avoid eternity without God, and become nice people who worship together with their families. But conversion starts a process of renewing our minds to become conformed to God's thought processes. Our pursuit of Christlikeness is referred to as discipleship. It's what Jesus announced as the church's comprehensive mission in the Gospel According to Matthew:

> Then Jesus came to them and said, "All authority in heaven and on earth has been given to me. Therefore, go and make disciples of all nations, baptizing them in the name of the Father and of the Son and of the Holy Spirit, and teaching them to obey everything I have commanded you. And surely I am with you always, to the very end of the age."
> **Matthew 28:18-20**

In New Testament terms, the gospel is the proclamation of the person and work of Jesus Christ. The Scriptures also detail how we appropriate those benefits to our soul and what it means to live out the gospel in a church community. But lest anyone misunderstand, people become Christians through a simple act of repentance and faith. The implication that someone must understand every implication of gospel living before becoming God's child is untrue. That type of thinking is the equivalent of the hyper-theologically minded person saying one can't become a Christian without first understanding advanced theology.

Nothing frustrates me more than academics who argue about what it means to be a Christian, or what the gospel is, when they've spent little time trying to explain the gospel to middle school kids. Jesus was glad that the Father had revealed Himself to little children and not the highly educated. When our gospel proclamation requires an advanced degree to experience conversion, we have a problem.[10] Scripture says that if we declare with our mouths that Jesus is the Christ and believe in our hearts that God raised Him from the dead, we will be saved. With our hearts we believe; with our mouths we profess our faith and are reconciled to God.[11] The apostle Paul gives a brief summary for the Corinthian church, which serves us well here:

"Now, brothers and sisters, I want to remind you of the
gospel I preached to you, which you received and on which
you have taken your stand. By this gospel you are saved, if
you hold firmly to the word I preached to you. Otherwise,
you have believed in vain. For what I received I passed
on to you as of first importance: that Christ died for our
sins according to the Scriptures, that he was buried, that
he was raised on the third day according to the Scriptures,
and that he appeared to Cephas, and then to the Twelve."

1 Corinthians 15:1-5

Certainly, there are varying aspects to the gospel message, including Jesus as King and the implications of being part of His kingdom. Understanding these notions is part of growing as a believer. However, one need not know all of these things before the Holy Spirit takes up residence in their soul. I knew nothing of mercy and justice as a young believer, but I became a Christian nonetheless and started pursuing God. Is there a necessary dimension to gospel living that includes working for mercy and justice? Absolutely. Is it a higher priority than growing in one's understanding of the life of Jesus and what God's Word teaches? No. But it's not a lower priority either. I don't believe that any single aspect of the church's mission is more important than the others.

In Acts 2:42-47, we read that the church had a multifold purpose, which included gospel outreach, meaningful relationships, corporate worship, study and application of the Scriptures, and community engagement. No one aspect of church life was more important than another. They're all part of being a disciple. Jesus has commanded us to be and to "make disciples." If we follow Christ, we must be disciplined students of our Lord, seeking to emulate His character and action in every area of our life. We're to see ourselves as part of His kingdom, which transcends earthly kingdoms and whose rule supersedes the rule of other kingdoms that we live in.

As to the tension between the church's vertical and horizontal dimensions and our involvement in social action, I ask this question? How many people have we talked to about Jesus's love and offer of salvation? Then, we need to ask how frequently we try to convince others (either in person or online) of our political or theological views? Most people are way more comfortable discussing politics than discussing their faith. I've known many theologically refined people who've never had a peaceful, friendly conversation with a nonbeliever about what it means to be a Christian. Often, they are concerned about offending someone (or being socially ostracized). However, if you were to check their social media platforms, you'd see great boldness about aligning with their political tribe.

I've discovered that it is far less threatening to sit around arguing theology with other Christians than to engage people so they can hear the gospel. It is much easier to march for my political cause than it is to mention my faith. I've marched for causes on both ends of the political spectrum. In all cases, there was a palpable sense of elation as I joined with others to protest. In those moments I always feel like my side is winning and that it won't be long until the struggle is over. A few days after the event, I usually return to reality and realize that as long as we're in human bodies, we will struggle. But when I'm with my political action crowd, holding my placard and chanting in unison, I feel bold and unafraid. Being part of a movement of people is intoxicating, and humanly speaking, it's empowering.

Being a countercultural Christian who follows a Jewish carpenter you believe came back to life? That can be a lonely road to travel. Christians who believe that only those who trust in Jesus Christ as Savior receive God's free gift of eternal salvation are a minority in the West. Statistics show that even among self-identified evangelical Christians, there is a significant portion that don't believe that Jesus is the only means of forgiveness of sin, and most believe human beings are, by nature, mostly good.[12] Therefore, holding to biblically defined doctrines will push you into a smaller demographic group. What's my point? Knowing what you believe is more important than ever. Especially if you hope to "Never leave the path." Before you publicly identify as a Christian, make sure you believe the doctrines of your faith.

A QUICK NOTE ABOUT IDENTITY

The West is now experiencing an identity crisis. What I mean is that identity politics is front and center and it's dominating our conversations. For the Christian, there needs to be gospel clarity about this issue, and there is. We look at identity through the lens of the risen Savior, who is seated at the right hand of the Father. Every Christian's primary identity is as a citizen of Christ's kingdom. Scripture teaches that our citizenship is in heaven and we should eagerly anticipate the return of King Jesus.[13] Regardless of what nation or tribe we're from, all of our secondary identifications must be subservient to our membership in God's royal family. This means that we prioritize emulating Jesus and living by His commands, even at the cost of our secondary identities.

A gospel identity means that we see all areas of our life as following the lead of King Jesus. If you identify as a Democrat or a Republican, you should consider yourself a Christian Democrat or Christian Republican. A Christian with a secondary political identity aligns all of their political practices with Scripture. If they can't do that, they speak up in opposition to that component of their coalition's platform. This isn't semantics. There is a real difference between a "political party Christian" and a Christian who is part of a political party. The former sees Christianity as a means to their end. The latter views politics as a means to seeing God's glory displayed in the world.

Genuine believers don't have the luxury of saying we're Christ followers who support the unjust killing of people or the economic oppression of countries or people groups. We shouldn't say that we're 100-percent onboard with our political party, because our political party is not Christ's party. Nor is it His mission. Our involvement in human institutions must be shaped by Scripture, which sometimes puts us on the outside looking in. Those are the costs of following

Christ. Our primary identity defines our other associations, and this has profound implications. If you place the Christian part of who you are behind something else, your Christianity will most certainly evolve and shift to align with your highest priority.

A CLEAR VIEW OF THE HEAVENS

In 1990, NASA launched the space shuttle Discovery, and in its payload was the long-anticipated Hubble Space Telescope. Hubble was created to enable scientists to get clear pictures and data from deep space. Telescopes work by using curved mirrors to gather light from the night sky. The shape of the mirror focuses the light, which is what we see when we look into the telescope lens. Because Hubble's mirrors were enormous, the amount of light (and therefore data) it could collect would provide a view into the cosmos that was unimaginable.

> **Our primary identity defines our other associations, and this has profound implications. If you place the Christian part of who you are behind something else, your Christianity will most certainly evolve and shift to align with your highest priority."**

However, when Hubble relayed its first pictures from deep space, they were blurry. The telescope's primary mirror was ground incorrectly by 1/50th of the width of a human hair, which resulted in a spherical aberration that compromised its capabilities. It wasn't that the flawed mirror completely distorted reality, as Hubble's initial Wide Field Planetary Camera sent back clear pictures of the universe. These images, however, could have been produced by a telescope on earth.

A team from the Jet Propulsion Laboratory in Pasadena, California, went to work to fix the problem. They placed four nickel-sized corrective mirrors inside of a new Wide Field Planetary Camera. Three years later, a space shuttle mission switched the cameras, and the rest, as they say, is history. Essentially (even though telescopes are all about mirrors) the Hubble was essentially fitted for a pair of contact lenses that corrected its vision. A relative who worked on this project said that when the first pictures from the corrected telescope arrived, we were able to see the glory of God's creation in ways we never believed possible. Because of NASA and JPL, the world would never be viewed the same way.

We've spent the past three chapters trying to bring clarity to the subjects of the gospel's message, our motives for following God, and the church's mission. The good news is that Jesus has come to clarify what was once a distant reality. For example, pre-Hubble scientists could see faraway planets and speculate about what was happening in and around them. But their understanding lacked detail. Something was missing. This wonderful space telescope now brings astounding clarity about the cosmos's scope and beauty. For Christians, Jesus has done the same for our understanding of who God is and what life is about.

Jesus's disciple Philip said to Him, "Show us the Father, and it is enough for us." Jesus replied, "Have I been with you so long, and you still do not know me, Philip? Whoever has seen me has seen the Father."[14] Jesus also told His followers that He and the Father were one.[15] And the Book of Hebrews begins by declaring gloriously:

> "In the past God spoke to our ancestors through the
> prophets at many times and in various ways, but in
> these last days he has spoken to us by his Son, whom
> he appointed heir of all things, and through whom also
> he made the universe. The Son is the radiance of God's
> glory and the exact representation of his being (my
> emphasis), sustaining all things by his powerful word.
> After he had provided purification for sins, he sat down at
> the right hand of the Majesty in heaven."
> **Hebrews 1:1-3**

Ancient philosophers made educated guesses about God's existence, the afterlife, and God's attributes, but their picture of God was fuzzy and speculative. The Hebrews had the benefit of God's partial revelation of Himself in the Old Testament, but it didn't contain the details that humanity craved. The New Testament says that while the Old Testament provides a glorious picture of God, the view Christ provides us is *incomparably* glorious.[16] Just as the Hubble and subsequent generations of space telescopes give us new clarity about the glory of the heavens, Christ's divinity allows Christians to declare that, that through Jesus, we can clearly see God as never before. With astounding clarity, we can see God's love, justice, and holiness through the incarnation of His only begotten Son, Jesus Christ. We're not speculating or making educated guesses about what used to be far away to human understanding. The risen Christ has made clear the glory of God.

For Christians, Jesus Christ enables our lives to be grounded in truth. Tip #3 for life on the narrow trail is, "Don't lose sight of the path." Because Jesus bodily resurrected from the dead, His claims of eternal existence are validated.[17] In fact, confidence in the historical reality of Jesus's resurrection is one of the reasons why I have confidence that the Old and New Testaments are inspired by the Holy Spirit and the revealed Word of God. This may sound like circular reasoning, but I don't think it is. I will explain why.

TIP #3 – Don't lose sight of the path
Spiritual confidence deepens with gospel clarity.

CONCLUSION

Why follow these tips?

I don't think there has ever been a more attractively titled television show than Bear Grylls' *Man vs. Wild.* The moniker alone makes me want to go on a safari and learn how to fish. Bear is a real-life James Bond. A former SAS Serviceman (the British equivalent of the Navy SEALs), he now shares his survival skills with the rest of us in TV land. Men want to be him, and women want to be with him. But Bear Grylls is a humble Christian man, so he'd likely defer any praise to his Savior. Having watched many episodes of his programs, I memorized a piece of advice that came in handy once.

In violation of Tips #1 and #3 for hiking, I once hiked by myself and wandered, losing sight of the path. I got turned around, but it was mid-day and I wasn't too far from home, so I wasn't that worried. And I recalled Grylls's advice to anyone who became lost in the wilderness: Go downhill until you find a stream. Follow the stream until you reach a river. Follow the river until you reach a road. The road will take you home. Do you know that this formula really works? (Consider this lifesaving tip a free bonus from me and Bear Grylls.)

Here's the difference between Bear's tips and the Three Tips* paradigm. His tips are for people who get lost in the physical world; this book is an attempt to prevent you from getting spiritually lost in the first place—and to help your soul find its way home. Why follow these Three Tips? I would love to say that they flow from my personal fount of wisdom, but I can't. I'm also unable to claim that I've always followed them perfectly. (Otherwise, I'd be proudly writing about how you should trust me, and that would violate Tip #2). Unfortunately, my wisdom was gained through a lot of foolishness and ignoring of the Scriptures. These "Three Tips" are valuable because they come from God's holy, inspired Word: The Bible. How do we get lost spiritually? We cease using God's Word as our guide. We follow our instincts in a dark universe. We quit looking to the heavens for guidance, as one would look to Polaris in the night sky.

Polaris, the North Star, appears stationary in the universe because it is positioned close to the line of Earth's axis, projected into space. It is the only bright star whose position relative to a rotating Earth does not change. All other stars appear to move opposite to the Earth's rotation. We live in a spiritually dark world, and naturally speaking, we operate without a compass. Most human beings navigate life's wilderness by their human instincts instead of using a constant like the North Star. From time immemorial, trackers and sailors have used Polaris as their true north. As long as you can see the North Star, you can head in the right direction.

For the Christian, God's Word is our spiritual North Star. One psalmist called it a lamp unto our feet and a light unto our path.[1] Jesus said that hearing and obeying His Word is the foundation of a secure life.[2] Paul said Scripture is breathed out by God and useful in teaching, confronting, correcting, and training in godliness.[3] The writer of the book of Hebrews proclaimed God's Word as living and active, sharper than a two-edged sword, powerful enough to surgically cut into our soul and call us to follow Jesus more faithfully.[4] God's Word is a sword of truth that we use to cut down the spiritual lies that shout misinformation and discouraging thoughts to us.[5] R.C. Sproul wrote, "I think the greatest weakness in the church today is that almost no one believes that God invests His power in the Bible. Everyone is looking for power in a program, in a methodology, in a technique, in anything and everything but that in which God has placed it—His Word."[6]

HOW CAN I BE CONFIDENT IN GOD'S WORD?

For many Christians, particularly those who are young in the faith, there is little understanding of why orthodox Christians consider God's Word, the Bible, to be inspired and trustworthy—the final authority for faith and practice. Before we conclude this book about spiritual health, it is important that you know why God's Word is trustworthy, powerful, and authoritative for the Christian.

Biblical scholar Craig Blomberg writes:
"Many people today harbor the notion that the distinctively Christian Scriptures collected together as the New Testament can hardly be trusted in what they teach. Ironically, there has never been more

evidence readily available that actually supports their reliability."[7]

The resources at our disposal provide ample scholarship addressing the concerns that critics of the New Testament have. While I am not a Biblical scholar, I did graduate from seminary and I have also studied a fair bit during my decades as a pastor. However, I am not an expert on this challenging topic. Accordingly, at the end of this book I have recommended some books and links to videos that provide scholarly discussion on the matter, which hopefully will provide you an opportunity to study for yourself.

What I would like to do is provide for you a snapshot of why I have confidence in Scripture. There are others who approach Scripture differently that I do, but my initial confidence begins and ends with the person of Jesus and his resurrection. It is true that we are told about the resurrection from Scripture. One could be accused of circular reasoning by saying, "I believe in the resurrection of Jesus Christ because of the Bible's testimony about the resurrection of Jesus Christ." But my confidence in the likelihood of the resurrection comes from a logical argument external to the Bible.

In his classic book *Loving God*, former Watergate conspirator Chuck Colson described the fragile nature of a high-level conspiracy. As President Richard Nixon's chief legal counsel, Colson was one of several who participated in the cover up of the administration's effort to bug the Democratic National Committee offices. Even though the inner circle of Nixon aides was highly educated and affluent, when pressured with the threat of lengthy prison sentences, they all abandoned their co-conspirators and saved their own skins. Colson said it was because they were the authors of the lie. Accordingly, they were not willing to go to prison to defend it, and certainly not willing to die for it. Colson wrote:

> "Take it from one who was inside the Watergate web
> looking out, who saw firsthand how vulnerable a
> cover is. Nothing less than a witness as awesome as
> the resurrected Christ could have caused those men to

maintain to their dying whispers that Jesus is alive
and Lord."[8]

One might contend that people die for lies all the time, and I would agree. Vulnerable people who are misled by powerful (sometimes religious) leaders have been convinced to take their lives in ritual suicide. However, I am unaware of any examples of a group conspiracy to perpetuate a lie, where all of those who fabricated the truth were themselves willing to die for their fiction. A single person might be willing to go down to protect their own legacy, but the likelihood of all of Jesus Christ's disciples being willing to suffer or die for their consciously invented deception is almost nonexistent. This is especially true because those who claimed they saw the resurrected Christ went on to promote a faith that required great personal sacrifice. If I were going to invent a religion, like many others before me, I would put myself at the head and make sure I received lots of creature comforts. Not so with the first century Christian martyrs. They lived lives of sacrifice to the end, and the majority Jesus's disciples died for their faith.

Therefore, I have reasonable faith in the resurrection of Jesus based on the unlikelihood of a mass conspiracy to perpetuate a fraud, where the participants were willing to die for their own lie. My confidence in Scripture is bolstered by my supposition that the historical figure Jesus Christ did come back to life. As a result, the written testimony of those who saw him bolsters my faith that the Holy Spirit did guide the writing and inspiration of Scripture.

True, my confidence in Scripture hangs on the supposition that Christ is alive. If he isn't alive, Christianity is a farce and the practice of praying to or worshipping a deceased human would be foolish. The alternative to Jesus Christ not being alive is that a group of men and women were either delusional or deceptive. In either of those two cases, Christianity is deservedly categorized as a hoax. Even the apostle Paul recognized the foolishness of Christianity if Jesus Christ did not genuinely rise from the dead.[9]

WHY I BELIEVE SCRIPTURE IS AUTHORITATIVE

While the issues of text reliability and authorship are challenges to work through, I believe there are answers for those tough questions. However, trusting God's Word to guide us is another issue altogether. Giving Scripture the authority to direct our lives requires that we actually believe that the Holy Spirit has breathed His inspiration through human authors. I want to share why I believe the Old and New Testaments are the revealed Word of God, and the final authority about what I believe and how I practice my faith.

First of all, if you consider the words of the New Testament to be historically reliable accounts of what Jesus taught, He clearly believed that the Scriptures were more than human words. In His earthly ministry, He repeatedly cites the Old Testament as the prophetic and authoritative Word of God. In His ministry debut at His home synagogue in Nazareth, Jesus reads from the prophet Isaiah and declares, "Today this scripture is fulfilled in your hearing."[10]

Another example of His vote of confidence in Scripture was when Jesus was led into the desert to be tempted by Satan. In response to these demonic lies, the Messiah quoted God's Word. Aside from using it as His weapon against evil, Jesus cites a verse from the Old Testament, one declaring the importance of God's Word for our spiritual nourishment: "It is written: 'Man shall not live on bread alone, but on every word that comes from the mouth of God.'"[11] And when summarizing God's law in response to a trick question from the Pharisees, Jesus proclaimed we're to "love the Lord your God with all your heart and with all your soul and with all your mind.' This is the first and greatest commandment. And the second is like it: 'Love your neighbor as yourself.' All the Law and the Prophets hang on these two commandments."[12] It's clear that the text of the New Testament shows our Savior's belief that the Old Testament was God's authoritative Word. It's also evident that early Christianity adopted His high view of its divine origin.[13]

As a young Christian, one practical question I had to face was, *how could human authors produce a divinely authoritative document if* they were imperfect? I've found a helpful answer to that question in the upper room discourse from the Gospel of John. On the night Jesus was betrayed, He declared to the disciples that when the Holy Spirit came, He would remind them of everything Jesus taught and guide them into all truth. This unique authority was granted to Jesus's disciples, many of whom would become the New Testament version of the Old Testament prophets that the Savior regularly quoted.[14]

Further, as I have surmised that Jesus did rise from the dead, then the claims of authority that Scripture makes about itself ring true to me. If Jesus is really alive and seated at the right hand of the Father, Christians could then have confidence that the Holy Spirit did proceed from the Father and the Son (in the words of the Nicene Creed) and breathed His words through the apostles to write the New Testament. If Jesus is really alive, and the Holy Spirit has genuinely come, we can have confidence that the apostles would be divinely enabled to accurately chronicle what Jesus said and did.

Again, presuming that the New Testament is historically reliable, it is also evident from the Scriptures that the apostles were aware of the authority given to them to dispense God's Word. John the Apostle wrote the Gospel of John, the Book of Revelation, and three letters that are included in the New Testament. Of all of those, I imagine that John 3:16 is the verse most quoted from John (it's certainly seen the most on television sporting events). A close second for most often quoted is 1 John 4:8, which wonderfully declares that "God is love." What I find interesting about the fourth chapter of John's first letter is how confident he is about the authority given to the Apostles. Just two verses before the oft quoted verse eight, came these words:

> "You, dear children, are from God and have overcome
> them, because the one who is in you is greater than the
> one who is in the world. They are from the world and
> therefore speak from the viewpoint of the world, and the
> world listens to them. We are from God, and whoever
> knows God listens to us; but whoever is not from God

does not listen to us. This is how we recognize the
Spirit of truth and the spirit of falsehood."
1 John 4:4-6

John declares "We are from God." He states that if they knew God, they would embrace his teachings as from God. Further, if they didn't listen to his teaching, they weren't from God. That's a bold statement for John to make if he hadn't actually been commissioned by Jesus. John rejected the false teachers that had infiltrated the church because they were leading Christians astray. This wasn't arrogance on his part, but instead an awareness that the Lord had declared the apostles to be the authoritative, prophetic voice of gospel truth to the church. During the first centuries of Christianity, these writings were collected and confirmed as having the marks of Scripture. The unified early church wrote its creeds based on the assembled writings of the apostles. Within a few centuries of Jesus, church leadership had brought to an end the disputes about which books were included in the canon.[15]

I'd never expect anyone who didn't believe in Jesus's resurrection to use it as the lens through which they read and trusted Scripture. But I do not understand why anyone who believes in Christ's resurrection would choose not to. Apart from the work of the Holy Spirit guiding and empowering the apostles, how could we ever trust that the Gospels were what our Savior actually said? Jesus didn't write down what He taught; His disciples did. If they weren't trustworthy in writing the letters the church has considered Scripture, why should anyone trust them to have chronicled Jesus's words accurately in the Gospels? And if a person contends that they believe in the resurrection of Jesus Christ but have zero confidence in the New Testament, they will likely have to conclude that while Jesus did come back from the dead, He left His followers without clear guidance regarding issues of faith and practice.

There are some who are content to not know whether Jesus actually said what the New Testament records. For many of these people, the actual text of Scripture holds little if any moral authority beyond how they hear God mystically speak it to them in their souls. It becomes the Word of God when they subjectively feel they've encountered God through it.[16] The problem with this method is that it opens the door to a wide variety of unjust, subjective, and contradictory propositions that perhaps no one (theologically liberal or conservative) would agree would be consistent with Christianity. Inevitably, the person who picks and chooses what they believe is inspired by God has to ask the question, "How can I confidently celebrate the use of Scripture in some cases and reject it in others?"

God's truth doesn't change, but our understanding of it does. In the end, the Scriptures must be the final word when the Bible is clear about a subject. Does science say people don't come back from the dead? Yes. That is what theologians call "general revelation," or truth we learn by human observation. But "special revelation" (Scripture) says God does miracles and can bring people back from the dead. This was evidenced supremely in the resurrection of Jesus Christ. Something may be factually true in a human sense, but when one presupposes the existence of an all-powerful God, then the Almighty gets to determine if He wants to override the parameters of natural science. Did God create the world in six 24-hour periods (resting on the seventh)? Varying biblical interpretations abound. But could God create the world in six days? Yes. Or He's not God.

THREE QUICK PIECES OF ADVICE

Orthodox Christianity professes that God's Word, in its original writings, was breathed by the Holy Spirit and is the final authority regarding Christian faith and practice. This does not mean that every translation of the original Hebrew or Greek texts is guaranteed to be 100-percent in agreement. It takes serious academic rigor or reasonable trust in a plurality of reliable scholars to be confident that the translated words are properly understood. Even with all their differences, these varying translations still amount to reasonable and reliable renderings of the original Greek and Hebrew manuscript portions that we have.

Regarding the authority of Scripture, here are some words of caution as you investigate, listen, and invite others to discuss Christian belief and practice: Yes, we want to grow in our understanding of what Scripture says. But as Christian apologist Alisa Childers says, "There's a difference between us progressing in our understanding of the eternal truths of God, and those truths themselves evolving, changing and progressing."[17]

Here are three pastoral "heads-ups" for when someone might be steering you away from submission to God's Word.

First, be careful when someone asks, "Did God really say?" as they try to get you to violate something you know is a biblical command. If that question sounds familiar, it's because those were the serpent's words for Adam and Eve in the Garden of Eden. Often, when we choose to ignore Scripture, it's because we've already decided we're not going to change our mind, even when confronted with correcting information. There is a substantial difference between the questions, "Does Scripture really say this?" and "Does God really say this?" The first is an inquiry about what God's authoritative Word actually says. The second is questioning the wisdom of God's Word as a pretext to ignoring it.

Second, beware of anyone who attempts to differentiate between the words of Jesus in Scripture from the words of the apostles. The apostles chronicled the words of Jesus. It's worth repeating: If those apostles weren't authoritatively guided by the Holy Spirit to write their letters to the churches, they weren't inspired by the Spirit to accurately remember Jesus's words in the Gospels. After we've done serious study, there may be nonessential issues we see a bit differently. But we have entirely left the Christian worldview when we eliminate the complete authority of God's Word. Even the apostle Peter (an uneducated fisherman) found some things Paul said hard to understand, but he sternly warned about twisting any Scripture (which he believed Paul's letters to be) to suit your own purpose.

"*Bear in mind that our Lord's patience means salvation, just as our dear brother Paul also wrote you with the wisdom that God gave him. He writes the same way in all his letters, speaking in them of these matters. His letters contain some things that are hard to understand, which ignorant and unstable people distort, as they do the other Scriptures, to their own destruction. (my emphasis) Therefore, dear friends, since you have been forewarned, be on your guard so that you may not be carried away by the error of the lawless and fall from your secure position.*"
2 Peter 3:15-17

Finally, beware of anyone who defines God's attributes (justice, love, mercy) differently than Scripture does. If Jesus always demonstrates love, then we have to see His driving the money changers from the temple and his confrontation of the greedy rich young ruler as motivated by and consistent with love. It IS loving to gently confront addicts who are killing themselves with drugs or plead with friends and family who are destroying their lives and families with their sexual promiscuity. It is loving to confront individuals who perpetuate systems of injustice, both for those who are being harmed and the oppressor themselves. If not, we need to quit protesting injustice altogether, because our actions are not loving.

A FINAL WORD

I made it home from my trek up Mount Wilson, but I was sore for two days. My friend Chris and I had climbed to the top, taken a picture, lain on the ground for thirty minutes, and then hiked three hours down the mountain. Not bad for a couple of middle-aged men. Recalling that accomplishment inspires various emotions. First, there many times when I felt like giving up. Second, I'm glad I did this with a friend. We share a bond now, and I needed his encouragement to continue on our climb. Finally, the experience reaffirmed the spiritual nature of all three hiking tips I'd received:

Never go alone.
Know your limitations.
Don't lose sight of the path.

Spiritually, we cannot make it on our own. We need others who trust God's Word and are committed to following Jesus in every area of their lives. We cannot experience authentic Christian friendships and church community unless we know the power of humbly sharing our weaknesses. We will never want to love God unless we are completely secure in the knowledge that He loves us, has forgiven us in Christ, and will never leave us.

May God bless and keep us as we live by the truths of His Word.

"We will never want to love God unless we are completely secure in the knowledge that He loves us, has forgiven us in Christ, and will never leave us."

RESOURCES FOR FURTHER STUDY OF SCRIPTURE'S RELIABILITY

BOOKS

Richard Bauckham, *Jesus and the Eyewitnesses: The Gospels as Eyewitness Testimony* (Grand Rapids: Wm. B. Eerdmans Publishing, 2017).

Craig L. Blomberg, *The Historical Reliability of the New Testament* (Nashville: B & H Publishing, 2016).

D.A. Carson, ed., *The Enduring Authority of the Christian Scriptures* (Grand Rapids: Wm. B. Eerdmans Publishing, 2016).

John M. Frame, *The Doctrine of the Word of God* (Phillipsburg: P & R Publishing, 2010).

Greg Gilbert, *Why Trust the Bible* (Wheaton: Crossway Publishing, 2015).

Craig S. Keener, *Miracles: The Credibility of the New Testament Accounts* (Grand Rapids: Baker Publishing, 2012).

Michael J. Kruger, *Canon Revisited: Establishing the Origins and Authority of the New Testament Books* (Wheaton: Crossway Publishing, 2012).

VIDEO

Is The Original New Testament Lost? A Dialogue with Dr. Bart Ehrman & Dr. Daniel Wallace
www.chuckryor.com/concl01 (https://www.youtube.com/watch?v=kg-dJA3SnTA&ab_channel=ehrmanproject)

Michael Kruger: God's Word in the Early Church
www.chuckryor.com/concl03 (https://www.youtube.com/watch?v=u2F0Kp-CjgM)

Encountering Challenges to Biblical Inerrancy
www.chuckryor.com/concl04 (https://www.youtube.
com/watch?v=wja4JmjIx60&feature=emb_title&ab_
channel=DallasTheologicalSeminary)

Why is the Bible reliable? Tim Keller at Veritas
www.chuckryor.com/concl05 (https://www.youtube.com/
watch?v=UZAPFKXMy_Y)

ABOUT THE AUTHOR

Dr. Chuck Ryor (PhD) is a professor of communication and a pastor, having planted two thriving church communities in Florida and California. He's currently the Lead Pastor of THE CHAPEL at Pasadena, which is part of the Harbor Network of churches. A graduate of Florida State University, Reformed Theological Seminary, and West Virginia University, Chuck and his wife of over three decades live in southern California.

Chuck blogs at www.chuckryor.com. For information about Chuck Ryor Ministries, email info@chuckryor.com.

ACKNOWLEDGMENTS

Thank you to the team of people that helped me with this book. In alphabetical order: Brenden, Brett, Brooks, Carolyn, Christine, Dean, Franzine, Isaiah, Jay, Jenny, Jon, Lynne, Melissa, Scott, Steven, and Todd.

I'm grateful for my friends and family. Thank you for showing me God's love. I'm especially thankful to my fellow elders from THE CHAPEL at Pasadena for their trust and encouragement. Finally, thank you to Tom Dean for leaving no stone unturned.

ENDNOTES

Introduction

[1] St. Augustine's *Confessions* (Lib 1,1-2,2.5,5: CSEL 33, 1-5).

[2] Eugene Peterson, *The Pastor: A Memoir* (New York: HarperCollins, 2011).

[3] Robert Robertson, *Come, Thou Fount of Every Blessing*. Public domain.

[4] Christina Zhao, "NBC's Chuck Todd Faces Backlash for Highlighting Letter Comparing Bible Story to Trump Falsehoods and 'Fairy Tales'," *Newsweek*, December 29, 2019, www.chuckryor.com/refi-4 (https://www.newsweek.com/nbcs-chuck-todd-faces-backlash-highlighting-letter-comparing-bible-story-trump-falsehoods-1479569).

Chapter One

[1] "About," America's Navy, www.chuckryor.com/ref01-1 (https://www.navy.com/seals).

[2] Jim Gaffigan, *Mr. Universe*, (August 28, 2012), 25:00.

[3] C.S. Lewis, *Mere Christianity* (New York: Touchstone, 1996), 109-112.

[4] Geert Hofstede, *Culture's Consequences: International Differences in Work Related Values* (Beverly Hills: SAGE, 1980), 125.

[5] "A.W. Tozer, *The Pursuit of God* (Camp Hill: Christian Publications, 1982), 22.

[6] Psalm 119:14, "*I praise you because I am fearfully and wonderfully made.*"

[7] 1 Timothy 2:3-4, "*This is good, and pleases God our Savior, who wants all people to be saved and to come to a knowledge of the truth.*"

[8] 2 Corinthians 5:10, "*For we must all appear before the judgment seat of Christ, so that each of us may receive what is due us for the things done while in the body, whether good or bad.*"

[9] Philippians 2:3-4, "*Do nothing out of selfish ambition or vain conceit. Rather, in humility value others above yourselves, not looking to your own interests but each of you to the interests of the others.*"

[10] Miroslav Volf, *After Our Likeness: The Church as the Image of the Trinity* (Grand Rapids: William B. Eerdmans Publishing Company, 1998), 173.

[11] Matthew 12:20, "*A bruised reed he will not break, and a smoldering wick he will not snuff out, till he has brought justice through to victory.*"

[12] John Stott, *The Message of 1 & 2 Thessalonians* (Sheffield: InterVarsity Press, 1991), 122.

[13] Jude 1:22, "Be merciful to those who doubt."

[14] Larry Crabb, *The Safest Place on Earth* (Nashville: Thomas Nelson, 1999), 37.

[15] 1 Corinthians 12:27.

[16] Psalm 139:23-24, "Search me, God, and know my heart; test me and know my anxious thoughts. See if there is any offensive way in me and lead me in the way everlasting."

[17] Hebrews 10:19-39.

[18] Benjamin Snyder, "7 Insights from Legendary Investor Warren Buffett," CNBC, May 1, 2017, www.chuckryor.com/ref01-18 (https://www.cnbc.com/2017/05/01/7-insights-from-legendary-investor-warren-buffett.html).

[19] Shuang Liu, Zala Volcic and Cindy Gallois, *Introducing Intercultural Communications* (London: SAGE, 2011), 248-249.

Chapter Two

[1] Ephesians 1:13-14, "And you also were included in Christ when you heard the message of truth, the gospel of your salvation. When you believed, you were marked in him with a seal, the promised Holy Spirit, who is a deposit guaranteeing our inheritance until the redemption of those who are God's possession—to the praise of his glory."

[2] Pew Research Center, "Why America's 'nones' don't identify with a religion," August 8, 2018, www.chuckryor.com/ref02-2 (https://www.pewresearch.org/fact-tank/2018/08/08/why-americas-nones-dont-identify-with-a-religion).

[3] Matt Carroll, Sacha Pfeiffer, and Michael Rezendes, "Church allowed abuse by priest for years," *The Boston Globe*, January 6, 2002, www.chuckryor.com/ref02-3 (https://www.bostonglobe.com/news/special-reports/2002/01/06/church-allowed-abuse-priest-for-years/cSHfGkTIrAT25qKGvBuDNM/story.html).

[4] John 13:34-35, "A new commandment I give to you, that you love one another: just as I have loved you, you also are to love one another. By this all people will know that you are my disciples, if you have love for one another."

[5] Jemar Tisby, *The Color of Compromise* (Grand Rapids: Zondervan, 2019), 49-50.

[6] John R.W. Stott, *The Cross of Christ* (Downers Grove: InterVarsity Press, 1986), 37.

[7] 1 Timothy 3:7, "He must also have a good reputation with outsiders, so that he will not fall into disgrace and into the devil's trap."

[8] AND Campaign, "Dr. Carl Ellis Jr—The Pimping Within Political Parties," YouTube Video, March 31, 2016, www.chuckryor.com/ref02-8 (https://www.youtube.com/watch?v=IQaleBGuhpg).

[9] Tim Keller, "How Do Christians Fit Into the Two-Party System? They Don't," *New York Times*, September 29, 2018, www.chuckryor.com/ref02-9 (https://www.nytimes.com/2018/09/29/opinion/sunday/christians-politics-belief.html).

[10] David French, "The Gospel of Life Is Clear: Virtuous Ends Do Not Justify Vicious Means," *The French Press*, May 10, 2020, www.chuckryor.com/ref02-10 (https://frenchpress.thedispatch.com/p/the-gospel-of-life-is-clear-virtuous).

[11] Timothy Dalrymple, "The Shepherd," *Christianity Today*, April 26, 2013, www.chuckryor.com/ref02-11 (https://www.christianitytoday.com/ct/2013/may/shepherd-michael-cromartie-faith-angle-forum.html).

[12] Michael Cromartie, interview by Chuck Ryor, November 21, 2014.

[13] David Masci, "Why Millennials are less religious than older Americans," Pew Research Center, January 8, 2016, www.chuckryor.com/ref02-13 (https://www.pewresearch.org/fact-tank/2016/01/08/qa-why-millennials-are-less-religious-than-older-americans/).

[14] Matthew 6:1, "*Be careful not to practice your righteousness in front of others to be seen by them. If you do, you will have no reward from your Father in heaven.*"

[15] Rachel Woodlock, Anthony Loewenstein, Jane Caro, and Simon Smart, "Doesn't religion cause most of the conflict in the world?" *The Guardian*, July 1, 2013, www.chuckryor.com/ref02-15 (https://www.theguardian.com/commentisfree/2013/jul/02/religion-wars-conflict).

[16] Alvin Schmidt, *How Christianity Changed the World* (Grand Rapids: Zondervan, 2001), 7.

[17] 1 Corinthians 5:1, 6:1, 11:21, 14:23. All four of these sections of Paul's first letter to the Corinthians highlight problem areas in the church.

[18] 1 John 4:19, "*We love because he first loved us.*"

[19] Brennan Manning, *Abba's Child* (Colorado Springs: NavPress, 1994), 3.

Chapter Three

[1] "Diarrhoeal Disease," World Health Organization, May 2, 2017, www.chuckryor.com/ref03-1 (https://www.who.int/news-room/fact-sheets/detail/diarrhoeal-disease).

[2] John McCain, "John McCain, Prisoner of War: A First-Person Account," *U.S. News & World Report*, January 28, 2008, www.chuckryor.com/ref03-2 (https://www.usnews.com/news/articles/2008/01/28/john-mccain-prisoner-of-war-a-first-person-account).

[3] Michael Horton, *Ordinary: Sustainable Faith in a Radical, Restless World* (Grand Rapids: Zondervan, 2014), 84.

[4] Carol Kuruvilla, "Televangelist Kenneth Copeland Defends His Private Jets: 'I'm A Very Wealthy Man,'" HuffPost, June 15, 2019, www.chuckryor.com/ref03-4 (https://www.huffpost.com/entry/kenneth-copeland-jet-inside-edition_n_5cf822fee4 b0e63eda94de4f).

[5] Acts 20:35, "In everything I did, I showed you that by this kind of hard work we must help the weak, remembering the words the Lord Jesus himself said: 'It is more blessed to give than to receive.'"

[6] 2 Corinthians 9:11, "You will be enriched in every way so that you can be generous on every occasion, and through us your generosity will result in thanksgiving to God."

[7] James 1:27, "Religion that God our Father accepts as pure and faultless is this: to look after orphans and widows in their distress and to keep oneself from being polluted by the world."

[8] Jeremiah 17:9, "The heart is deceitful above all things and beyond cure. Who can understand it?"

[9] Matthew 22:37-39, "Jesus replied: 'Love the Lord your God with all your heart and with all your soul and with all your mind.' This is the first and greatest commandment. And the second is like it: 'Love your neighbor as yourself.'"

[10] Dell Hymes, Foundations in Sociolinguistics: An Ethnographic Approach (Philadelphia: University of Pennsylvania Press, 1974), 3-9.

[11] John Owen, Communion with God (Edinburgh: Banner of Truth Trust, 1991), 137.

[12] Barbara Duguid, Extravagant Grace (Phillipsburg: R&R Publishing, 2013), 40.

[13] John 16:12-15, "I have much more to say to you, more than you can now bear. But when he, the Spirit of truth, comes, he will guide you into all the truth. He will not speak on his own; he will speak only what he hears, and he will tell you what is yet to come. He will glorify me because it is from me that he will receive what he will make known to you. All that belongs to the Father is mine. That is why I said the Spirit will receive from me what he will make known to you."

[14] Richard Foster, Celebration of Discipline (New York; Harper & Row Publishers, 1978), 151.

[15] Hebrews 13:5 referencing Deuteronomy 31:6, "Be strong and courageous. Do not be afraid or terrified because of them, for the Lord your God goes with you; he will never leave you nor forsake you."

[16] John 14:15-17, "If you love me, keep my commands. And I will ask the Father, and he will give you another advocate to help you and be with you forever—the Spirit of truth. The world cannot accept him, because it neither sees him nor knows him. But you know him, for he lives with you and will be in you."

[17] Proverbs 27:17, "As iron sharpens iron, so one person sharpens another."

Chapter Four

1 "Roger Mattson, Victor Stello and the Hydrogen Bubble," PBS, www.chuckryor.
com/ref04-1 (https://www.pbs.org/wgbh/americanexperience/features/three-roger-
mattson-victor-stello-and-hydrogen-bubble).

2 J.I. Packer, *Weakness is the Way* (Wheaton: Crossway Books, 2013), 15.

3 Matthew 6:13, "And lead us not into temptation, but deliver us from the evil one."

4 Charles Hodge, *Systematic Theology* (Grand Rapids: Baker, 1988), 289.

5 R.C. Sproul, "Cosmic Treason," *Tabletalk Magazine*, May 1, 2008, www.chuckryor.
com/ref04-5 (https://www.ligonier.org/learn/articles/cosmic-treason).

6 Sproul, ibid.

7 Psalm 51:5, "Surely I was sinful at birth, sinful from the time my mother conceived me."

8 Isaiah 53:6, "We all, like sheep, have gone astray, each of us has turned to our own way;
and the Lord has laid on him the iniquity of us all."

9 Alvin Plantinga, *God, Freedom, and Evil* (Grand Rapids: Eerdmans, 1977), 27.

10 Genesis 50:19-20, "But Joseph said to them, 'Don't be afraid. Am I in the place of God? You
intended to harm me, but God intended it for good to accomplish what is now being done,
the saving of many lives.'"

11 John 1:29, "The next day John saw Jesus coming toward him and said, 'Look, the Lamb of
God, who takes away the sin of the world!'"

12 "The Nicene Creed: Where it came from and why it still matters," Zondervan
Academic, March 9, 2018, www.chuckryor.com/ref04-12 (https://zondervanacademic.
com/blog/the-nicene-creed-where-it-came-from-and-why-it-still-matters).

13 Will Friedwald, "Sinatra vs. 'My Way,'" *Wall Street Journal*, June 2, 2019, www.
chuckryor.com/ref04-13 (https://www.wsj.com/articles/SB124389543795174079).

14 Scott Meslow, "Taking a Stand Against Frank Sinatra's 'My Way,'" GQ, August 13,
2016, www.chuckryor.com/ref04-14
(https://www.gq.com/story/my-way-is-the-worst).

15 John 15:5, "I am the vine; you are the branches. If you remain in me and I in you, you will
bear much fruit; apart from me you can do nothing."

16 1 John 5:14-15, "This is the confidence we have in approaching God: that if we ask
anything according to his will, he hears us. And if we know that he hears us—whatever we
ask—we know that we have what we asked of him."

17 Luke 6:27-29, "But to you who are listening I say: Love your enemies, do good to those
who hate you, bless those who curse you, pray for those who mistreat you. If someone slaps
you on one cheek, turn to them the other also."

Chapter Five

[1] John 6:44, "No one can come to me unless the Father who sent me draws them, and I will raise them up at the last day."

[2] Dan B. Allender, *Leading with a Limp* (Colorado Springs: WaterBrook Press, 2006), 55.

[3] Ben Sixsmith, "The sad irony of celebrity pastors," *Spectator USA*, December 6, 2020, www.chuckryor.com/ref05-3 (https://spectator.us/sad-irony-celebrity-pastors-carl-lentz-hillsong/amp/?__twitter_impression=true&fbclid=IwAR2A3PnhwEwsyR4lke_XaXqiCaKWjoKrSOeIEF_KkwwsuzujY04bnw8T_I8).

[4] Francis A. Schaeffer, *No Little People, No Little Places* (Wheaton: Crossway Books, 1974), 26.

[5] 1 Peter 5:6, "Humble yourselves, therefore, under God's mighty hand, that he may lift you up in due time."

[6] J.I. Packer, *Weakness is the Way* (Wheaton: Crossway Books, 2013), 53-54.

[7] Rachel Gilson, "My Same-Sex Attraction Has an Answer," *Christianity Today*, March 2, 2020, www.chuckryor.com/ref05-7 (https://www.christianitytoday.com/ct/2020/march-web-only/same-sex-attraction-has-answer.html).

[8] Chuck DeGroat, *When Narcissism Comes to Church: Healing Your Community From Emotional and Spiritual Abuse* (Downers Grove: InterVaristy Press, 2020), 107.

[9] James 5:16, "Therefore confess your sins to each other and pray for each other so that you may be healed. The prayer of a righteous person is powerful and effective."

[10] Susan Scutti, "The Psychology of Sycophants," CNN, December 22, 2017, www.chuckryor.com/ref05-10 (https://www.cnn.com/2017/12/22/health/psychology-of-sycophancy/index.html).

[11] Jen Kim, "So You Think You Can Be Famous?" *Psychology Today*, June 20, 2016, www.chuckryor.com/ref05-11 (https://www.psychologytoday.com/us/blog/valley-girl-brain/201606/so-you-think-you-can-be-famous).

[12] Rick Warren, *Rick Warren's Daily Devotionals*, Day 120, www.chuckryor.com/ref05-12 (https://www.bible.com/reading-plans/135-rick-warrens-daily-devotional/day/120).

[13] Henri J.M. Nouwen, *Out of Solitude* (Notre Dame: Ave Maria Press, 1974), 18.

Chapter Six

[1] Thomas Watson, *The Art of Divine Contentment* (Morgan: Soli Deo Gloria, 1853), 44.

[2] Philippians 2:3-4, "Do nothing out of selfish ambition or vain conceit. Rather, in humility

value others above yourselves, not looking to your own interests but each of you to the interests of the others."

[3] Ephesians 4:2, "Be completely humble and gentle; be patient, bearing with one another in love."

[4] Mother Teresa, A Simple Path (New York: Ballantine Books, 1995), 115.

[5] Micah 6:8, "He has shown you, O mortal, what is good. And what does the Lord require of you? To act justly and to love mercy and to walk humbly with your God."

[6] Matthew 26:10-13, "Aware of this, Jesus said to them, 'Why are you bothering this woman? She has done a beautiful thing to me. The poor you will always have with you, but you will not always have me. When she poured this perfume on my body, she did it to prepare me for burial. Truly I tell you, wherever this gospel is preached throughout the world, what she has done will also be told, in memory of her.'"

[7] See Acts 6:1-7 for a detailing of this early church "problem."

[8] Larry Hurtado, Destroyer of the Gods: Early Christian Distinctiveness in the Roman World (Waco: Baylor University Press, 2016), 183.

[9] 1 Corinthians 5:12, "What business is it of mine to judge those outside the church? Are you not to judge those inside?"

Chapter Seven

[1] John H. Leith, Creeds of the Churches: Nicene Creed History (Louisville: Anchor Books, 1963), 28-31.

[2] F.F. Bruce, The New Testament Documents: Are They Reliable? (Grand Rapids: William B. Eerdmans Publishing Company, 1960), 27.

[3] For the complete account of the receiving of Gentiles into the church, visit Acts 15:1-35.

[4] The 2019 Anglican Book of Common Prayer was interpreted and written by the Anglican Church in North America.

[5] "The State of Theology," Ligonier Ministries, March 2020, www.chuckryor.com/ref07-5
(https://thestateoftheology.com).

[6] Vern Poytress, "The Shadow of Christ in the Law of Moses" (Philippsburg: P & R Publishing Company), 65.

[7] John 15:13, "Greater love has no one than this: to lay down one's life for one's friends."

[8] John 1:29.

[9] Verses from Revelation 5:6, 5:8, 7:17, 14:4, 14:10, 15:3, 19:9, 21:23, 22:1, 22:3.

[10] Charles Hodge, *Systematic Theology* (Grand Rapids: Baker Book House, 1988), 397.

[11] John 3:16-18, "For God so loved the world that he gave his one and only Son, that whoever believes in him shall not perish but have eternal life. For God did not send his Son into the world to condemn the world, but to save the world through him. Whoever believes in him is not condemned, but whoever does not believe stands condemned already because they have not believed in the name of God's one and only Son."

[12] Elyse Fitzpatrick, *Found in Him* (Wheaton: Crossway Books, 2013), 95.

[13] Romans 3:28, Galatians 2:16, Philippians 3:9, and Romans 5:1 are just four of many Scripture verses that declare our salvation is not by our good works but instead through genuine faith.

[14] Romans 10:9, "If you declare with your mouth, 'Jesus is Lord,' and believe in your heart that God raised him from the dead, you will be saved."

[15] John 3:5, "Jesus answered, 'Very truly I tell you, no one can enter the kingdom of God unless they are born of water and the Spirit.'"

[16] John 15:15-17, "If you love me, keep my commands. And I will ask the Father, and he will give you another advocate to help you and be with you forever—the Spirit of truth. The world cannot accept him, because it neither sees him nor knows him. But you know him, for he lives with you and will be in you."

[17] See Acts 2 for a comprehensive recollection of the Pentecost experience of Christ's disciples.

[18] Exodus 40:34, "Then the cloud covered the tent of meeting, and the glory of the Lord filled the tabernacle."

[19] Matthew 12:20 and Isaiah 42:3, "A bruised reed he will not break, and a smoldering wick he will not snuff out."

[20] John 2:19-21, "Jesus answered them, 'Destroy this temple, and I will raise it again in three days.' They replied, 'It has taken forty-six years to build this temple, and you are going to raise it in three days?' But the temple he had spoken of was his body."

[21] Hebrews 1:3, "The Son is the radiance of God's glory and the exact representation of his being, sustaining all things by his powerful word. After he had provided purification for sins, he sat down at the right hand of the Majesty in heaven."

Chapter Eight

[1] James 2:14-19, "What good is it, my brothers and sisters, if someone claims to have faith but has no deeds? Can such faith save them? Suppose a brother or a sister is without clothes and daily food. If one of you says to them, 'Go in peace; keep warm and well fed,' but does nothing about their physical needs, what good is it? In the same way, faith by itself, if it is not accompanied by action, is dead. But someone will say, 'You have faith; I have deeds.' Show me your faith without deeds, and I will show you my faith by my deeds. You believe that there is one God. Good! Even the demons believe that—and shudder."

[2] James 5:16, "*Therefore confess your sins to each other and pray for each other so that you may be healed. The prayer of a righteous person is powerful and effective.*"

[3] 1 Peter 3:18, "*For Christ also suffered once for sins, the righteous for the unrighteous, to bring you to God. He was put to death in the body but made alive in the Spirit.*"

[4] The doctrine of the imputed righteousness of Jesus is referred to in 1 Peter 3:18.

[5] Romans 3:25-26, "*God presented Christ as a sacrifice of atonement, through the shedding of his blood—to be received by faith. He did this to demonstrate his righteousness, because in his forbearance he had left the sins committed beforehand unpunished—he did it to demonstrate his righteousness at the present time, so as to be just and the one who justifies those who have faith in Jesus.*"

[6] Genesis 3:1, "*Now the serpent was more crafty than any of the wild animals the Lord God had made. He said to the woman, 'Did God really say, You must not eat from any tree in the garden?'*"

[7] Scottish theologian James Buchanan's essays on "Grace and Works" have significantly shaped my understanding of this subject. In particular, Lecture VII, pg. 344 of the book collection titled *The Doctrine of Justification* (first published in 1867).

[8] Jerry Bridges, *Transforming Grace* (Colorado Springs: NavPress, 1991), 79.

[9] Galatians 5:22-23, "*But the fruit of the Spirit is love, joy, peace, forbearance, kindness, goodness, faithfulness, gentleness and self-control.*"

[10] Luke 6:45, "*A good man brings good things out of the good stored up in his heart, and an evil man brings evil things out of the evil stored up in his heart. For the mouth speaks what the heart is full of.*"

[11] Hebrews 4:15-16, "*For we do not have a high priest who is unable to empathize with our weaknesses, but we have one who has been tempted in every way, just as we are—yet he did not sin. Let us then approach God's throne of grace with confidence, so that we may receive mercy and find grace to help us in our time of need.*"

[12] Matthew 13:24-30. In the *New Bible Commentary*, D.A. Carson notes on this passage, "The weeds are probably darnel, which looks very much like wheat in the early stages of growth and after that is so closely entangled with it that it cannot be removed without damaging the wheat."

[13] John 1:1, "*In the beginning was the Word, and the Word was with God, and the Word was God.*"

[14] Hebrews 13:5, "*God has said, 'Never will I leave you; never will I forsake you.'*"

[15] John 13:23.

[16] Joseph Hart, "Come Ye Sinners, Poor and Needy" (1759), public domain.

Chapter Nine

[1] Monergism, "The Definition of the Council of Chalcedon (451 A.D.)," www.chuckryor.com/ref09-1
(https://www.monergism.com/definition-council-chalcedon-451-ad).

[2] Herman Ridderbos, *The Coming of the Kingdom* (Philadelphia: Presbyterian and Reformed Publishing Company, 1962), 186.

[3] Matthew 6:10.

[4] Revelation 7:9 says that before the throne of God there will be represented a collection of redeemed souls from every nation, tribe, people, and language.

[5] James 1:26-27, "Those who consider themselves religious and yet do not keep a tight rein on their tongues deceive themselves, and their religion is worthless. Religion that God our Father accepts as pure and faultless is this: to look after orphans and widows in their distress and to keep oneself from being polluted by the world."

[6] Ephesians 2:8-10, "For it is by grace you have been saved, through faith—and this is not from yourselves, it is the gift of God—not by works, so that no one can boast. For we are God's handiwork, created in Christ Jesus to do good works, which God prepared in advance for us to do."

[7] John 15:5.

[8] Helmut Koester, "The Great Appeal: What did Christianity offer its believers that made it worth social estrangement, hostility from neighbors, and possible persecution?", FRONTLINE, published April 1998, www.chuckryor.com/ref09-8
(https://www.pbs.org/wgbh/pages/frontline/shows/religion/why/appeal.html).

[9] Acts 6:7, "So the word of God spread. The number of disciples in Jerusalem increased rapidly, and a large number of priests became obedient to the faith."

[10] Matthew 11:25-26, "At that time Jesus said, 'I praise you, Father, Lord of heaven and earth, because you have hidden these things from the wise and learned, and revealed them to little children. Yes, Father, for this is what you were pleased to do.'"

[11] Romans 10:8-10, "But what does it say? 'The word is near you; it is in your mouth and in your heart,' that is, the message concerning faith that we proclaim: If you declare with your mouth, 'Jesus is Lord,' and believe in your heart that God raised him from the dead, you will be saved. For it is with your heart that you believe and are justified, and it is with your mouth that you profess your faith and are saved."

[12] "The State of Theology," Ligonier Ministries, September 8, 2020, www.chuckryor.com/ref09-12
(https://thestateoftheology.com).

[13] Philippians 3:20, "But our citizenship is in heaven. And we eagerly await a Savior from there, the Lord Jesus Christ."

[14] John 14:8-9.

[15] John 10:30, "I and the Father are one."

[16] 2 Corinthians 3:9-11, *"If the ministry that brought condemnation was glorious, how much more glorious is the ministry that brings righteousness! For what was glorious has no glory now in comparison with the surpassing glory. And if what was transitory came with glory, how much greater is the glory of that which lasts!"*

[17] John 8:58, *"'Very truly I tell you,' Jesus answered, 'before Abraham was born, I am!'"*

Conclusion

[1] Psalm 119:105, *"Your word is a lamp for my feet, a light on my path."*

[2] Matthew 7:24-27, *"Therefore everyone who hears these words of mine and puts them into practice is like a wise man who built his house on the rock. [25] The rain came down, the streams rose, and the winds blew and beat against that house; yet it did not fall, because it had its foundation on the rock. [26] But everyone who hears these words of mine and does not put them into practice is like a foolish man who built his house on sand. [27] The rain came down, the streams rose, and the winds blew and beat against that house, and it fell with a great crash."*

[3] 2 Timothy 3:16-17, *"All Scripture is God-breathed and is useful for teaching, rebuking, correcting and training in righteousness, so that the servant of God may be thoroughly equipped for every good work."*

[4] Hebrews 4:12, *"For the word of God is alive and active. Sharper than any double-edged sword, it penetrates even to dividing soul and spirit, joints and marrow; it judges the thoughts and attitudes of the heart."*

[5] Ephesians 6:17, *"Take the helmet of salvation and the sword of the Spirit, which is the word of God."*

[6] R.C. Sproul, *The Prayer of the Lord* (Sanford: Reformation Trust, 2009), pg. 100-101.

[7] Craig Blomberg, "The Reliability of the New Testament," The Gospel Coalition, www.chuckryor.com/refc-7 (https://www.thegospelcoalition.org/essay/reliability-new-testament).

[8] Charles W. Colson, *Loving God* (Grand Rapids: Zondervan, 1987), 69.9

[9] Corinthians 15:12-19, *"[12] But if it is preached that Christ has been raised from the dead, how can some of you say that there is no resurrection of the dead? [13] If there is no resurrection of the dead, then not even Christ has been raised. [14] And if Christ has not been raised, our preaching is useless and so is your faith. [15] More than that, we are then found to be false witnesses about God, for we have testified about God that he raised Christ from the dead. But he did not raise him if in fact the dead are not raised. [16] For if the dead are not raised, then Christ has not been raised either. [17] And if Christ has not been raised, your faith is futile; you are still in your sins. [18] Then those also who have fallen asleep in Christ are lost. [19] If only for this life we have hope in Christ, we are of all people most to be pitied.*
[10] Luke 4:21.

[11] Matthew 4:4.

[12] Matthew 22:37-40.

[13] Craig L. Blomberg, "Reflections on Jesus' View of the Old Testament" in *The Enduring Authority of the Christian Scriptures*, ed. D.A. Carson (Grand Rapids: William B. Eerdmans Publishing Company, 2016), 673.

[14] See John 14:25-26, John 15:26-27, John 16:7, and John 16:12-15 for the role of the Holy Spirit in guiding the disciples.

[15] Michael Kruger's book *Canon Revisited: Establishing the Origins and Authority of the New Testament Books* (Wheaton: Crossway, 2012) has been a reliable source for many regarding the history of establishing the New Testament.

[16] Norman L. Geisler and William E. Nix, *From God to Us: How We Got Our Bible* (Chicago: Moody Press, 1974), 27.

[17] Capturing Christianity, "Alisa Childers: 'Progressive Christianity is Dangerous,'" YouTube Video, May 25, 2020, www.chuckryor.com/refc-17 (https://www.youtube.com/watch?v-oQ6doQsSQLU).

A free ebook edition is available with the purchase of this book.

To claim your free ebook edition:

1. Visit MorganJamesBOGO.com
2. Sign your name CLEARLY in the space
3. Complete the form and submit a photo of the entire copyright page
4. You or your friend can download the ebook to your preferred device

Morgan James
BOGO™

A **FREE** ebook edition is available for you or a friend with the purchase of this print book.

CLEARLY SIGN YOUR NAME ABOVE

Instructions to claim your free ebook edition:
1 Visit MorganJamesBOGO.com
2. Sign your name CLEARLY in the space above
3. Complete the form and submit a photo of this entire page
4. You or your friend can download the ebook to your preferred device

Print & Digital Together Forever.

Snap a photo

Free ebook

Read anywhere